SAINT MICHAEL'S MOUNT

ST MICHAEL'S MOUNT

SAINT MICHAEL'S MOUNT

BY

THE REV. T. TAYLOR
M.A., F.S.A.
Hon. Canon of Truro

CAMBRIDGE
AT THE UNIVERSITY PRESS
1932

CAMBRIDGE UNIVERSITY PRESS
Cambridge, New York, Melbourne, Madrid, Cape Town, Singapore,
São Paulo, Delhi, Dubai, Tokyo

Cambridge University Press
The Edinburgh Building, Cambridge CB2 8RU, UK

Published in the United States of America by
Cambridge University Press, New York

www.cambridge.org
Information on this title: www.cambridge.org/9780521137966

First published 1932
This digitally printed version 2010

A catalogue record for this publication is available from the British Library

ISBN 978-0-521-13796-6 Paperback

To

*the Writer respectfully
Dedicates this
Book*

Contents

Preface	page ix
The Mount	1
Ictis	11
Religious History	21
The Priors	52
Humphry Arundell	91
Pilgrimage	100
The Corody at the Mount	108
Military and Civil	112
John de Vere, Earl of Oxford	121
Perkin Warbeck	133
Governors and Receivers of the Mount	144
Appendix I *Leofric's Grant of Freedom from Episcopal Control*	172
II *William of Worcester's Version*	172
III *In Laudem Michaelis et Angelorum Omnium*	173
IV *Manucaptors (with Index)*	176
General Index	197

ILLUSTRATIONS

St Michael's Mount   *Frontispiece*

Saint Michael the Archangel   *page* 28

The Mount in 1582   127
   (from Norden's *Speculi Britanniae*)

Heraldic shields:

    Pomeray   114

    Vere, Earl of Oxford   123

    Bloyou   145

    Harris of Hayne   155

    Cecil, Earl of Salisbury   161

    Basset of Tehidy   165

    St Aubyn, Lord St Levan   171

Preface

READERS of *The Celtic Christianity of Cornwall* may remember that, without expressing a definite opinion respecting the identity of Ictis, the writer was inclined to accept the late Mr Clement Reid's conclusion and to identify Ictis with the Isle of Wight. He no longer hesitates to declare his firm conviction that Ictis is St Michael's Mount. The *Legenda Aurea*, from which William of Worcester obtained the description which he attributed to St Michael's Mount, refers to Mont St Michel when it speaks of a place surrounded by a dense wood infested by wild beasts. The argument therefore founded on William of Worcester's description falls to the ground.

The conclusion arrived at by the present writer, the result of independent research, agrees with that of Mr T. A. Rickard as recorded in the *Journal of the Royal Institution of Cornwall*. In dealing with the subject he has accepted Mr Rickard's and Mr Reid's translations of classical authors, profited by their suggestions and desires to express his obligations to them. Had he read Mr Rickard's paper before entering upon his task he would have been spared much troublesome research. To Father Delehaye his acknowledgments are expressed elsewhere.

The papers contributed by Mr W. J. Blake to the same *Journal* have been useful in dealing with the rebellions of De Vere, Warbeck and Arundell.

The present writer has endeavoured, wherever possible, to give the *ipsissima verba* of the documents quoted and the references. This has doubtless somewhat hindered the steady flow of the narrative and necessitated a closer application on the part of the reader. The book professes to be history, not romance.

The writer has aimed at setting forth his story under two heads—Religious and Secular. Inevitably they intermingle and involve a certain amount of repetition. Of those who have written upon the subjects dealt with, three only have been accepted as authoritative—John Warkworth, Richard Carew and Polydore Virgil—and these only because they lived sufficiently near the time of the events they record.

A document of great interest is given in the Appendix. It furnishes the names of those who were mulcted in heavy fines for their supposed complicity in Warbeck's insurrection. No one, who is conversant with the unscrupulous methods employed by King Henry VII and his ministers in order to extort money from the king's subjects, will attach importance to the pretext put forward for the purpose; but all who are interested in genealogical research will be glad to avail themselves of the information which the document supplies in order to compare and correct the pedigrees entered by the heralds at a later period. The document embraces almost every parish and in many instances its chief landowner. For the convenience of those who wish to consult it the items have been numbered and indexed.

To his old friend and schoolfellow, the Rev. F. W. Paul, M.A., and Mr C. B. Buckland, B.Litt., of the Public Record Office, who have assisted, the former by revising some of the translations, the latter by direction and advice; to Miss Joan Wake for permitting the use of transcripts made at Hatfield, and above all to Lord St Levan, who has allowed him to examine and use the muniments in his possession and has permitted the dedication of the book to him—the author

> Can nothing render but allegiant thanks.

T. T.

ST JUST IN PENWITH
May 1932

The Mount

ST MICHAEL'S MOUNT has been described as picturesque. So it is. But in this case the epithet is poor and inadequate. It would be better to say that it is an achievement. The mighty forces which piled up the gigantic rock more than 250 feet above the sea level, left it solitary, somewhat shattered but nevertheless solid, steadfast and enduring; an object to wonder at and explore, a place to use for commercial enterprise so soon as the old world began to learn the use of metals, a refuge for hermits in search of solitude and self-knowledge, a home for monks living in community who required buildings for shelter and devotion, a castle to guard and to be guarded in time of war. As one epoch succeeded another some trace was left marked upon its rugged features, some sign to betoken its chequered fortunes. The most wonderful thing about the Mount is the way in which in all its parts man has co-operated with nature to produce a perfect and harmonious whole. As viewed from every point on the mainland it is difficult to determine where nature's work ends and man's begins, so intimate and complete is their correspondence. St Michael's Mount is an achievement, unconscious, to some extent no doubt on man's part; but closer examination only serves to reveal the same steady process at work. Nothing artificial or bizarre, no sign of neglect jars upon the sense. The conies still sport on the green sward as in the days of Leland,

the praises of God still ascend to God in the church
built in the fourteenth century, and the flag granted
by Charles II still floats from its tower. Royal personages, distinguished soldiers and sailors, statesmen
and bishops, English and Orthodox, receive a welcome at the Mount. There is no edifice in Cornwall or
perhaps in the west of England with such a wealth of
tradition, so arresting in its natural beauty and so
wisely and warily preserved.

Here it is only possible to indicate some of the
more prominent features of the pile of buildings
which crown the summit of the great rock. Leland
shall be our guide.

The south-south-east of the Mount is pasturable and
breedeth conies; the residue is high and rocky....The way
(from the mainland) to the Church entereth at the north side
from half-ebb to half-flood tide to the foot of the Mount
and so ascendeth by steps and greces westward and then re-
turneth eastward to the outer ward of the church. Within the
said ward is a court strongly walled wherein on the south side
is the chapel of St Michael and in the east side the chapel of
our Lady. The captains' and the priests' lodgings be in the
north side and the west of St Michael's chapel.

The ascent from east to west is by a comparatively
narrow pathway strongly protected by a curtain of
rock on the right hand, running parallel with it in the
middle of the hill, and at its western extremity, by a
barricade constructed of rock with embrasures and a
sentry-box at the angle where it turns to the left.
Until modern times this was the only means of

approach to the church and castle. No knowledge of military operations is needed to convince the onlooker how strongly fortified was the Mount against attack until the use of high explosives was discovered.

The worship of Almighty God has been celebrated here for over a thousand years, and it is impossible to say how many times it has been necessary to provide a fresh building for the purpose. The church dedicated by Bishop Warelwast in 1135 is stated to have been levelled with the ground by an earthquake which took place in the year 1275.[1] It is remarkable, however, that no record of this catastrophe is to be found in the Episcopal Registers which are complete from the year 1258 and record the appointment of Robert Carteret to the priory in 1266 and his successor Richard Perer in 1276.

The present church was built sometime during the fourteenth century, probably towards the end of it. The ring of bells, hereafter described, was cast for the tower between the years 1385 and 1408, and in 1433 Sir John Arundell bequeathed a sum of money towards the construction of the rood screen[2] which was removed early in the eighteenth century. Dr Borlase, writing in the year 1730, gives the following description of it: "The Church is a nave divided by the cancelli or lattice work of the rood loft into an

[1] Annales de Waverleia—A.D. 1275 Item. iii idus Septembris, inter horam diei primam et tertiam, factus est generalis terrae motus per universam regionem, cujus impetu Ecclesia quae dicitur Sancti Michaelis de Monte solo cecidit complanata.

[2] Lego operi cancellariae faciendae.

aisle and a choir. The Rood loft was carved and painted with the history of the passion and not inelegantly for former times".

The same Sir John Arundell bequeathed a similar sum of money towards the maintenance of the "light of St Michael". He had held, in 1418, the king's commission to serve at sea with three knights, 364 men-at-arms and 1776 archers, and doubtless had cause to bless God and St Michael for the beacon on the church tower. A bequest for the same purpose is found in the will of Peter Bevill, Esq., which was proved in 1515. The lantern, octagonal in shape, of very hard stone, is situated at the south-west angle of the embattled parapet of the tower and, being no longer required as a receptacle for the beacon light, has become associated with the good or evil fortune of newly married couples, the first, bride or bridegroom, to reach it and to be seated in it after the marriage ceremony, acquires henceforth supreme control of domestic affairs. The real St Michael's Chair is a craggy tor in the west part of the island, and is described by Norden as "somewhat dangerous for access". The interior of the church affords evidence of wise and discriminating judgment in the preservation of essential features and their adaptation to modern conditions. In calling attention to some of its more striking features we cannot do better than follow Dr Borlase who, in 1730, wrote as follows: "In the choir there were three stalls on each side of the entrance and at the altar two tall eastern windows with a rose one at the finishing of the top and, besides the three windows on each side of the nave of tolerable Gothic fashion, a handsome rose window at the western end".

The two rose windows mentioned by him are a joy to behold, the glass being of that resilient and radiant brightness associated with the Tudor or *cinque cento* period.

Of Tudor date are three of the nine panels of the reredos which the late Lord St Levan caused to be inserted in it. Of these the three referred to are of English and the remaining six of French workmanship of a later date. The central panel is of great beauty and represents St John Baptist's Head in a charger with the Three Persons of the Holy Trinity above, St James and St Christopher on either side, and Our Lady, St Thomas of Canterbury and St Peter below. The subjects of the other two English panels are: on the north side, St Gregory's Mass, and on the south side Pilate washing his hands. The subjects of the French panels have been identified as Susanna and the Elders, the Three Kings (two panels), the Washing of St Peter's Feet, the Sacrifice of Isaac, and the Sop given to Judas.

Towards the end of the fifteenth century Nottingham became famous for artistic work in alabaster obtained from the deposits of that mineral in Derbyshire. It is probable that here we have some of the best specimens of it.

The central panel intrigues one to ask why was St John Baptist chosen for a subject? St John is the patron of the Knights Hospitallers and his head appears on the reverse side of the Maltese coinage. The Knights Hospitallers were, until 1539, the patrons of the living of Madron, and in the fourteenth century the services in the chapel of St Mary, Penzance, were shared between the Prior of St Michael's Mount and the Vicar of Madron.[1]

Much has been written concerning the underground chamber which is entered by means of a stone stairway from the south-west of the altar. The vault is about nine feet square and has a small square-headed window now blocked, in the south wall. This chamber may have served as an *in pace* cell such as existed at Mont St Michel for the correction of refractory monks and others. When laying the floor of the chancel there was found in it the skeleton of a very large man uncoffined. The bones were removed and interred in the north court. In 1864 they were translated to the cemetery. The shin bone was larger by one-half than that of an ordinary man.

There are also seven large seventeenth-century silver candlesticks; two of them, of English craftsmanship, are of great beauty and said to be unique; the remaining five, less beautiful, are said to be of Spanish make.

A fourteenth-century cross richly carved let into the balustrade leading to the north door of the church is well worthy of study. The head of the cross has four pinnacles and between them in sculptured recesses are carved: (1) the Virgin and Child, (2) a Pilgrim or Monk, (3) the Crucifixion, (4) a King.

[1] Chan. Inq. p.m. 15 Edward II, No. 49.

The chapel of Our Lady, which now forms an integral portion of the castle buildings and is furnished as such, is situated in the east side of the court, side by side with the church, and is described by William of Worcester in 1478 as newly built. It took the place of an earlier chapel the furniture of which is described in the inventory of 1430.

Of the six bells five were procured for the tower towards the close of the fourteenth century and dedicated in the usual manner. The names given to them were chosen from the heavenly hierarchy and commemorate those five orders of angels which in the Liturgy are found in the daily Preface[1] to the Sanctus, wherein the worshipper is invited to unite with them in his tribute of praise to God. The five orders are Angels, Dominations, Powers, Virtues and Seraphin. As explained elsewhere in this book, the Manual of Voragine, Archbishop of Genoa, known as the *Legenda Aurea* (founded upon that of pseudo-Dionysius who lived in the seventh century), was in use at the Mount when William of Worcester paid his visit in 1478. When naming the bells the prior appears to have reckoned Michael among the Thrones[2] one of the highest orders of the hierarchy.

---

[1] Per quem majestatem tuam laudant *Angeli,* adorant *Dominationes,* tremunt *Potestates.* Coeli coelorum que *Virtutes,* ac beata *Seraphin,* socia exultatione concelebrant. *Sarum Missal.* The English Prayer Book version gives a singularly beautiful rendering of this Preface but does not specify or differentiate the several offices performed by the Angels and Archangels.

[2] See page 27 where this economy is explained.

Dr Borlase fortunately preserved an account of the bells as he found them in the eighteenth century. They were then five in number, and of them the fifth, or tenor, had been recast in 1640 and bore coin impressions of that date. In 1785 the second bell was broken up and two others (now the second and third) substituted for it. The original inscription on this bell was "Sancte Nicholae: Ora pro nobis; Ordo Principatuum". The third and fourth (now the fourth and fifth) bear the cross of William Ffounder who has been identified with William Dawe, a London founder (1385–1408). The capital letters are Lombardic. As already stated the tenor bell has been recast. There can be little doubt that it originally bore the name of St Michael, the patron of the church. The ring would therefore be somewhat as follows:

1. ✠ Ordo Potestatuum

2. Sancte Nicholae Ora Pro Nobis

    Ordo Principatuum

3. Spiritus Sanctus Est Deus ✠ Gabriel
   Sancte Paule Ora Pro Nobis

    Ordo Virtutum Maria

4. Filius Est Deus ✠ Raphael
   Sancta Margarita Ora Pro Nobis

    Ordo Archangelorum

5.   (Pater Est Deus)
            (✠ Michael)

St Nicholas whose name was invoked on the second bell is the patron of sailors, and St Margaret the patroness of women in childbirth.

Of the new bells the second bears the legend "Come away make no delay" (1785), the third "Charles and John Rudhall Fe(cerunt)", the sixth "soli Deo Debetur gloria 1640".

The main entrance to the castle is by a doorway surmounted by the St Aubyn arms, from that ward in the west described by Leland of which the only traces which remain are fragmentary walls north and south. The recent removal of plaster inside the door has disclosed the grooves of the portcullis and suggested the contrivances by which it was raised and lowered.

The castle itself is a great pile of buildings closely compacted, strongly and securely joined together so as to form a charming and convenient habitation. The most interesting room is the refectory of the monks now known as the "chevy chase" room, from the frieze which adorns it and which represents scenes of hunting of various beasts and birds. The frieze is thought to have been placed here by John St Aubyn, Esq., in the reign of Charles II, who made the castle his place of residence. Dr Schwertz however who has made a study of the subject maintains that the frieze is not later than the sixteenth century. Over the fireplace at the east end of the room is a panel with the arms of Charles II, and at the west end panels with the arms of St Aubyn and Godolphin. John St Aubyn married Catherine, daughter of Francis

Godolphin of Trevaneage. He died in the year 1684, and from him the present owner of the Mount, Lord St Levan, is descended.

A Glastonbury chair in the "chevy chase" room of uncertain date is worthy of notice. Upon it is carved the legend

> Johannes Arthure
> Monachus Glastonic
> Salvet eū Deus
> Sit laus Deo
> Da pacem Dñe

The drawing room is spacious and leaves nothing to be desired. On its walls are valuable paintings, mostly portraits of the more distinguished members of the St Aubyn family, some of them by Opie, and among others the well-known portrait of Barbara Duchess of Cleveland by Sir Peter Lely. In every room may be found objects of interest and value collected from all parts of the world by members of the St Aubyn family.

Those who are interested in the study of ichthyology will find a vast and valuable assortment of fishes in the rectangular museum near the entrance to the Mount.

Ictis

So much has been written concerning Ictis, the island whence tin was exported in ancient days to the Mediterranean, that it is impossible to omit all reference to it in a work which attempts to describe St Michael's Mount and its history. The question before us is briefly this: Was Ictis the island now known as St Michael's Mount?

On the one hand we have eminent geologists and archaeologists like the late Mr Clement Reid and Mr Reginald Smith who have maintained that Ictis is identical with Vectis, the Isle of Wight; on the other hand, we have the patriotic consensus of considered opinion which has recently found expression in the person of Mr F. A. Rickard[1] that Ictis is the Cornish Mount.

Mr Clement Reid based his conclusion upon an interpretation of a passage taken from Diodorus Siculus and the erosion of the isthmus which 2000 years ago is supposed to have joined the Isle of Wight to the mainland: Mr Rickard upon a somewhat different interpretation of the said passage, and a comprehensive survey of the history of the tin trade of Britain with the Mediterranean.

The earliest mention of trade with western Europe is to be found in the Bible. Solomon's ships went to Tarshish, 1000 B.C., with the servants of Hiram, King of Tyre, once every three years, and brought

[1] *Journ. Roy. Inst. of Cornwall*, XXII, 201–51 (A.D. 1927).

back gold, silver, ivory, apes and peacocks.[1] Jehosha-phat, King of Judah, joined with Ahaziah, King of Israel, 896 B.C., and made ships to go to Tarshish. Tarshish was Tartessus, a city and province on the western coast of Spain. The prophet Ezekiel (588 B.C.) in his lament over Tyre tells us: "Tarshish was thy merchant by reason of the multitude of all kind of riches: with silver, iron, tin, and lead, they traded in thy fairs".[2]

Herodotus (450 B.C.) is the first classical author who speaking from personal knowledge says:

> Of the western extremities of Europe I cannot speak with certainty, for I do not admit that there is a river called by the barbarians Eridanus that empties itself into the northern sea, whence, it is said, the amber comes, nor am I acquainted with the islands called the Tin Islands (Cassiterides) from whence we are said to get our tin (kassiteros)...however, both tin and amber come to us from those remote parts.

He does not say how these two commodities were brought, but leaves us to imply that they both arrived in the same way. The Baltic was doubtless the source of the amber.

From the days of Herodotus until the days of Julius Caesar we have no contemporary evidence of the tin trade in the west. Caesar (56 B.C.) informs us that "the Britons use bronze and gold money and iron rings of fixed weight. The provinces remote from the sea produce tin, and those upon the coast iron, but the latter in no great quantity. Their bronze is all

---

[1] 2 Chron. ix. 21.   [2] Ezekiel xxvii. 12.

imported". Caesar landed on the south-east coast and presumably knew little of the south-west.

We have now to consider the testimony of several writers who lived subsequent to the Christian era. Two of them were contemporary and wrote during the first quarter of the first century. Both were indebted to Posidonius, who was born in Syria in the year 135 B.C., and died at Rome at the age of eighty-four. The two writers referred to are Diodorus Siculus and Strabo. The former's statement has been the subject of much discussion and may be given *in extenso*.[1] He says:

The inhabitants of Britain who live in that part of Britain which is named Belerion are very fond of strangers, and, owing to their intercourse with merchants, civilised in their manners. They prepare the tin, working very carefully the earth in which it is produced. The ground is rocky, but it contains veins of earth the produce of which is ground down, smelted and purified. They beat the metal into masses, shaped like astragali (knuckle bones), and carry it to a certain island lying off the coast of Britain called Ictis. During the ebb of the tide the ground between is left dry, and they carry over into the island the tin in abundance in their waggons. Now there is a peculiar phenomenon connected with the neighbouring islands, I mean those that lie between Europe and Britain, for at the flood tide the intervening passage is overflowed and they seem like islands; but a large space is left dry at the ebb and then they seem like peninsulas. Here, then, the merchants buy the tin from the natives and carry it over to Gaul; and after travelling

[1] *Archaeologia*, IX (2), 282; *Journ. R.J.C.* XXII, 204.

overland for about forty days they finally bring their loads on horses to the mouth of the Rhone.

Tin is found in many parts of Iberia (Spain), not being discovered on the surface as some have babbled in their histories, but dug and smelted like silver and gold. For beyond the land of the Lusitanians (Portugal) are many mines of tin in the islands that lie off Iberia in the Ocean, which on this account are called the Cassiterides. And a great deal is brought from the British island also to that part of Gaul that lies opposite; and across the midlands of the Celtic country it is brought on horseback to the people of Massilia (Marseilles) and to the town called Narbona. This is a colony of Romans which because of its fitness and its wealth is the greatest place of exchange in those regions.

Contemporary with Diodorus was Strabo, the geographer of Pontus, who tells us that the Cassiterides are ten in number which lie near each other in the ocean north of the haven of the Artabri on the north coast of Spain. After describing the natives he states that they trade in tin, lead and skins, and that in former times the Phoenicians alone carried on the traffic from Cadiz (Gades), concealing the passage from everyone until an adventurous Roman following a trading vessel was wrecked and only escaped with his life by clinging to a fragment of his ship. In spite of this disaster the Romans eventually discovered the passage, and Publius Crassus, who became Caesar's legate to Gaul in 58 B.C., arranged for amicable trade by sea with the natives.

There is only one point in his narrative which is perplexing, viz. his concluding statement that the sea route is longer than that to Britain. He may mean that the distance by sea from the Mediterranean port to the Cassiterides is greater than that from the Cassiterides to Britain. It must be remembered that both Diodorus and Strabo got much of their information from Posidonius, who lived a century earlier.

Separated by half a century from Diodorus and Strabo we come to Pliny the Elder who perished in the great eruption of Mount Vesuvius in the year 79. Pliny states that "six days' sail inward from Britain there was an island named Mictis on which white lead (tin) was found, and to this island the Britons came in boats of osier covered with sewn hides".

He is quoting from the historian Timaeus who lived in the fourth century before Christ. Our minds naturally recall the Ictis of Diodorus, and Vectis, the Roman name of the Isle of Wight. Nevertheless it is only by regarding them as different places that we can piece together the several statements above given and other statements bearing on the subject.

When Pliny speaks of a six days' passage inwards from Britain he surely means a voyage of six days towards the place of discharge, that is Mictis, whence the tin was to be forwarded to the Mediterranean. Mr Clement Reid and others identify Mictis with the Isle of Wight; but Mr Rickard very pertinently asks why go to the Isle of Wight overland by roads which presented almost insurmountable obstacles, when by means of one tack they could round the Isle of Ushant and aided by the prevailing west wind arrive at the

mouth of the Loire without difficulty? By going to
the Isle of Wight the ship master would more than
double his labour, for he would have to beat down
channel against the wind.

In the days of Timaeus (353–326 B.C.) there was,
of course, no overland traffic from the northern ports
of Gaul to the Mediterranean. Wherever Mictis may
have been situated, it was, according to Timaeus, six
days' sail from Britain. And therefore it could not
have been the Ictis spoken of by Diodorus which was
at ebb tide a peninsula of Britain. The Scilly Isles do
not answer this description, which are less than one
day's sail from Land's End. If we suppose Mictis to
have been one of the islands on the west coast of
Brittany we shall probably be little short of the mark.
We may even go so far as to identify those islands
with the Cassiterides.

The Phoenicians were unquestionably the greatest
navigators of the ancient world. They were the first
to pass beyond the Straits of Gibraltar. In the eighth
century B.C. they founded Gadir (Cadiz). Spain was
valuable to them for the sake of its tin. The demand
for the metal could hardly have remained unknown
for long to the natives farther north. It is not unlikely that they brought their quota to Cadiz. It is
impossible to say whether the Phoenicians themselves ever got beyond the Spanish peninsula. No
traces of Phoenician culture have been discovered
either in Gaul or Britain. Two notable voyages of
exploration may be mentioned. Hamilco of Carthage
at the beginning of the sixth century B.C. is stated by

Pliny to have sailed into the English Channel; and in 325 B.C. Pytheas, a Greek of Marseilles, was sent by the merchants of that city to discover the source of amber. Skirting the coast of Kent Pytheas penetrated as far as the mouth of the Vistula in the Baltic. Soon afterwards the overland trade route from the mouth of the Loire to Marseilles was opened up, and the supply of tin from Britain was delivered at or near the mouth of that river.

Having introduced the subject of Phoenician tin traffic, concerning which there has been so much controversy, the reader is entitled to know what conclusions the writer has formed on the subject. That the Phoenicians of Tyre founded Gades (Cadiz) for the purpose of the tin trade there is little doubt; but that they traded directly with Britain there is insufficient evidence. Their successors, the Carthaginians, in the fourth century B.C., appear to have transferred the tin market from Gades to the mouth of the Loire, and to have carried the ore overland and by river to Marseilles. In both cases they received the ore or metal from the natives of the tin producing regions, who brought it to them by sea or raised it in the neighbourhood. There is no convincing evidence that the Carthaginian merchants came to Britain. Even if we assume that Diodorus is quoting Posidonius, the merchants who in the second century B.C. bought the tin at Ictis were neither Phoenician nor Carthaginian. *Delenda est Carthago*. Its destruction was accomplished in 146 B.C. If we suppose Ictis not to be identical with Mictis—the present writer's contention—then there is good reason to conclude that Ictis was St Michael's Mount.

In order to grasp fully the significance of this result and its implications it becomes necessary to consider it in the light of William of Worcester's account of the Mount written in the year 1478. William tells us that the second apparition of St Michael took place in Tumba in *Cornwall*, formerly called "Hore-rok in the Wodd", which is an exact translation of the Cornish term applied to it by Camden and others, viz. *Karrik luz en Kuz*, otherwise *Carreg lowse en Cowse*. It is not therefore surprising that modern writers should have been led to the conclusion that within historic memory the Mount was a precipitous rock surrounded by a forest.

In order if possible to discover the special commemorations of St Michael at the Mount on the various days assigned to the archangel the present writer, suspecting that the fourth apparition described by William as *in ierarchiis nostrorum angelorum* was an extract from the lection used at such commemorations, after a diligent search was, through the courtesy of an eminent hagiologist,[1] enabled to identify it. It is taken from the *Legenda Aurea* of James à Voragine, a Dominican friar of the thirteenth century, who in the year 1292 became archbishop of Genoa. As will be explained later, the passage is a disquisition upon the angelic hierarchy and therefore of little value for our present purpose except to assure

[1] R. P. Delehaye, S.J., Director of the Société des Bollandistes, Brussels.

us that Tumba was situated six miles from the city of Avranches. An examination of Caxton's English Translation and Mabillon's *Acta Sanctorum* was more illuminating. Caxton states that the apparition was "in a place which was named Tumba by the see syde sixe myle fro Cyte dauverances" (city of Avranches). Mabillon, a Benedictine of immense learning who lived in the seventeenth century and obtained his information from an anonymous writer who lived soon after the Apparition in Tumba, certainly before the year 960, and also from the *Legenda* in use in the abbey of St Germain des Prés, written at the command of Adrald the Abbot in 1060, describes Tumba as six miles from Avranches and goes on to say we have learnt from these and other reliable authorities that "formerly it was enclosed by a very dark wood six miles from the mouth of the sea, affording very well-found lurking places for wild beasts (*opacissima silva claudebatur...altissima praebens latibula ferarum*)". Now these are almost the very words William of Worcester uses of St Michael's Mount (*opacissima primo claudebatur sylva...altissimam praebens latebram ferarum*). It seems certain therefore that all four writers had recourse to a common source for their information, and that their description of Tumba was that of the Norman and not the Cornish Mount. It is moreover generally admitted that before the year 709 the description would exactly correspond with the results of historical and scientific research.[1] How

[1] Vide *L'Histoire et l'Architecture de Mont St Michel*, by Paul Gout, pp. 2–25.

then are we to account for the phrase "Hore-rok in the Wodd" used by William of Worcester to describe St Michael's Mount? There is no need to assume a deliberate intention to deceive. It is not unlikely that during the two-and-a-half centuries which had elapsed from the time of the severance of the Cornish from the Norman Mount the same *Legenda* was used at both places, and that, wittingly or unwittingly, the passage which described the archangel's appearance in Tumba was interpreted and explained to the people as having reference to the former. Be that as it may, the phrase was misapplied and the main support of the Isle of Wight's identification with Ictis falls to the ground. It is therefore tolerably safe to assume that Ictis, the island-peninsula of Diodorus, was the place which since the days of Edward the Confessor has been known as St Michael's Mount in Cornwall.

Religious History

IT is impossible to say at what particular period the Mount began to be used for religious purposes. From its general character and situation, so closely resembling the islets near the coasts of Brittany, Ireland, Wales and elsewhere, which in prehistoric times were places of sepulture and therefore sacred, and subsequently the habitations of hermits and monks, one would naturally conjecture that the Cornish Mount had a similar history. This supposition receives support from a statement in Camden's *Magna Britannia*[1]—whether the statement be Camden's or that of one of the editors of his work is of no consequence in this connection—that "at the bottom of this Mount, within the memory of our fathers, as they were digging for tin, they found spear-heads, battel-axes and swords of copper, all wrapt up in linen, of the same sort as those discovered long ago in Hircinia and lately in Wales".

The Bronze Age is well represented in West Cornwall and, although comparatively little is known respecting the religious worship of the men of that period, there has been discovered in Gaul and elsewhere sufficient evidence to warrant us in attributing to them worship of the Sun.[2] A manuscript of late twelfth-century date,[3] referring to a saint who is

[1] Vol. i, p. 309, ed. 1720.
[2] Déchelette, *Bronze Age*, chap. xiii.
[3] Cott. MS. Vesp. A, xiv.

supposed to have lived in the sixth century, states that St Michael's Mount was distinguished and called, in the language of that province, Dinsol. One is tempted to suggest "hill of the sun" as its equivalent. The first syllable is Old Celtic and the last Latin unless we suppose the second syllable to be *sul*, the name of a goddess who gave her name to Bath (*Aquae Sulis*).

Composite words (Old and Late Celtic, Celtic and Latin, Celtic and English) are not unknown in Cornwall (e.g. Caerdin *hodie* Kerthin, Penpont and Roscommon) and it is possible that in Dinsol we may have the hill or citadel of the sun and an echo of sunworship. A recent explanation has been put forward, which discredits the Cottonian MS. entirely, and identifies Dinsol with Denzell, a farm in St Mawgan in Pydar, a few miles from Padstow, where St Cadoc, with whom the manuscript is concerned, had a chapel and well. The manuscript may be briefly paraphrased: When St Cadoc had come from St Michael's Mount which is known to be in Cornwall and is called in the idiom of that province, Dinsol, where the archangel is venerated by all who come to him here, hot with his journey and tired, he was exceedingly thirsty and thereupon struck his staff into the parched soil and procured water for himself and those who were with him. A six-mile walk could hardly warrant an expedient so expensive. Capgrave also mentions the visit of St Cadoc to St Michael's Mount and the miracle, but omits to say that it was known also by the name of Dinsol. In the *Acta Sanctorum* under October 8th, it is stated of St Keyne that, after many years had elapsed, when the fame of the holy virgin had become widely known and she had been visited by many at the oratory, St Cadoc in his travels, visiting St Michael's Mount, found his mother's sister, St Keyne, there and was filled with great joy; and when he would have led her back to her own land he was not permitted to do so by the people of the place (*terrae*).

The name of St Cadoc appears to have been preserved in Lescudjack (Cadoc's court) and, in default of a better derivation, St Keyne may have given her name to Kenegie.

As a place of abode for a Celtic hermit before the castle was built and a settlement established at its foot, no place more suitable could be imagined. The hermit instinctively sought seclusion and, if possible along with it, some useful occupation as road-mender, bridge-repairer or light-keeper. It is no mere fancy which pictures the hermits of Chapel Carn Brea, St Michael's Mount and Rame Head as light-keepers. When monks—members of a community—succeeded solitaries, they would naturally take over their duties. This had probably occurred at the Mount before the Norman Conquest. Duke Richard of Normandy had substituted Benedictine monks for priests at Mont St Michel about the middle of the tenth century,[1] but no such change had been made at the Mount. In the days of Edward the Confessor it was held by Brismar the priest.[2]

[1] Mabillon, *Annales Benedictini.*
[2] Domesday Book.

The Cornish Mount bore the name of St Michael before the Norman Conquest.[1] The Norman abbey had been founded to commemorate St Michael's appearance to Aubert, Bishop of Avranches, in the eighth century. The building of its magnificent abbey church was begun by Richard, Duke of Normandy, in the year 966 and finished by his son, William the Conqueror.

The early years of the last English king, St Edward the Confessor, were spent in Normandy where he

> ...loved the holy company
> Of people of religion
> Who loved only that which was good;
> Especially a monk who led
> A high and heavenly life.

In Normandy Edward acquired a culture and a sense of dignity which were all but unknown to his English subjects. He had a natural taste for architecture and cultivated it. As the founder of the abbey church and palace of Westminster he gave it expression.[2] He had doubtless watched the patient and persistent efforts of the builders of the Norman monastery at Mont St Michel and the steady rise of its walls. On the death of Hardicanute in 1042 he ascended the throne of his forefathers. England was in a state of disorder and Edward was not fitted, either by nature or by education, to cope with the lawlessness and

[1] Most of the hills of Cornwall were under the archangel's invocation, e.g. Roughtor, Rame Head, Caerhayes, etc.

[2] Bp. Creighton, *Historical Essays*.

political intrigue of a people who had got completely out of hand. His interests were centred in social and religious reform. He introduced into England a higher standard and a stricter sense of justice, and for centuries he lived in men's minds as a national saint and hero. Although he could have had but a general interest in Duke Robert's enterprise, it seems not unlikely that the contemplation of it may have suggested to him a similar foundation on the great rock in Mount's Bay. Be that as it may it is certain that, if we accept his charter as genuine, he granted or confirmed to St Michael and the brethren serving God in that place the lands of Amaneth, i.e. Meneage. Moreover the paragraph in Domesday Book referring to the Mount is entitled *St Michael of Cornwall*, and states that in the days of King Edward it was in the hands of Brismar the priest, and that its demesne, the manor of Truthwall, then consisted of two hides of land which had never paid geld.

The Celtic ideal of a monastery was that of a missionary college into which were received postulants of all sorts and conditions, and in which children were taught the rudiments of education and trained for the religious life. In Wales, Llantwit, and in the west of England, Glastonbury were the most famous. It is noteworthy that John of Glastonbury,[1] in his description of the relics preserved at Glastonbury, mentions *inter alia* those of Saints Rumon, Corentin (Cury), Winwallo, Hilary, Budock, Samson,

---

[1] *Chronica sive Historia de Rebus Glastoniensibus,* ed. Thomas Hearne, 1726.

Tudwal and Petrock. It would therefore seem that, at a very early period, some sort of link was formed between that abbey and West Cornwall.

Like the Benedictine, the Celtic monasteries were originally independent of each other, although all probably observed the same or a similar rule. There was no central authority exercising control over the several communities. Possibly the link between the Lizard Saints and Glastonbury was something like that which subsists between the alumni of a university and their Alma Mater. Those who had won distinction were commemorated, not all together on the same day or in the same way, but on different days—the days of their deaths. During the period between Athelstan and William the Conqueror, if not earlier, there appears to have been the welding together of separate interests under a central authority and the recognition of it by Edward the Confessor.

The worship of St Michael is supposed to have been derived by the Jews from Chaldea. He was accepted as Israel's prince and heavenly protector after the captivity. In the time of Constantine the Great this worship, using the word in its widest sense, which had been forbidden by the Church, was allowed and spread rapidly throughout the East. In the West it began at a somewhat later date. Three appearances (*apparitiones*) of St Michael are recorded. The first is said to have taken place at Mount Garganus or Gorgan in Apulia in the fifth century; the second at the castle of St Angelo in the days of St Gregory the Great who became pope in the year 590;

and the third at or near Mont St Michel in the year 710.

William of Worcester who visited Cornwall in the year 1478 and wrote an account of his visit, entitled *Itinerarium sive liber Rerum memorabilium*, and who obtained much of his information from the regular and secular clergy and attended mass at St Michael's Mount on September 17th in that year, gives, doubtless as the result of enquiries made on the spot, many interesting particulars concerning it, loosely scattered throughout his ill-arranged note-book.

William gives the three apparitions, but inverts the order of the second and third. A fourth apparition (*in ierarchiis ipsorum angelorum*) mentioned by him, as already stated, afforded the key to the source whence he obtained his information. The words quoted are the introduction to a learned and elaborate disquisition concerning the various orders of angelic beings and the ministrations assigned to them, illustrated by references to Holy Scripture and other writings. Here it must suffice to say that there are three triads in the celestial hierarchy, viz. Cherubim, Seraphim and Thrones; Dominations, Virtues and Powers; Princedoms, Archangels and Angels. To each of these orders are assigned offices of greater or less importance according to their degrees of dignity.[1]

The estimation in which the Archangel Michael was held in the sixteenth century is illustrated by an epigram of Erasmus (1467–1536), sometime Lady

[1] An admirable description of this economy will be found in Mrs Jamieson's *Sacred and Legendary Art*, II, 87–100.

Margaret Professor of Divinity at Cambridge, the friend of Dean Colet and Sir Thomas More, and still more widely known for his edition of the Greek Testament with a Latin translation. In his epigram Erasmus greets the archangel as the captain-general

SAINT MICHAEL THE ARCHANGEL

of the armies of heaven; the divinely appointed arbiter of human merit with the power of life and death; the guardian of devout souls; the angel whom St John saw in vision holding the golden censer and offering clouds of incense with the prayers of saints to God; the vanquisher of that old serpent, the devil, whose aspect is described with terrifying precision;

the refuge for women in distress and the guardian and bedesman of those harassed by war; one whose prayers Erasmus beseeches in order that days of rejoicing may be given when peace is restored to weary lands.[1]

When all due allowance has been made for poetical imagery, the epigram doubtless reflects the popular and accepted tribute paid to the archangel and the wide range of his activities.[2]

Readers of Domesday Book will have been struck with the description of the land-holders of the hundred of Pawton, who held of St Petrock, and the close correspondence between them and the land-holders of Winnington (Kerrier), who held of the Count of Mortain. They are described as "thegns who could not be separated from the manor". There were seventeen of these thegns at the Lizard in the reign of Edward the Confessor who held lands in Winnington, and these lands were geld-free and, in this

[1] See Appendix 1.

[2] A very curious and amazing legend is given in the *Legenda Aurea* which the reader will perhaps prefer to have in the writer's words and language: "In eodem loco (Monte St. Michaelis) quoddam memoria dignum contigisse refertur miraculum. Ille enim mons undique Oceano cingitur, sed bis in die Sancti Michaelis iter praebens populo aperitur. Cum ergo copiosa turba ad ecclesiam pergeret, contigit et quandam mulierem gravidam vicinamque partui secum ire. Et ecce magno impetu unda rediit et omnis turba timore perculsa ad littus fugit, sola autem mulier praegnans fugere non valuit, sed a marinis fluctibus capta fuit. At Michael archangelus mulierem servavit illaesam, ita etiam, quod in medio pelagi filium parturivit quem in ulnis suscipiens lactavit, et mari iterum sibi iter praebente cum puero laeta exivit".

respect also, resembled those of St Petrock. In Cornwall freedom from the payment of geld was characteristic of monastic lands. Not only so, a large portion of the Lizard peninsula, in the Conqueror's day, already bore the name of Amaneth or Meneage, that is, monastic land. When, therefore, we find Edward the Confessor granting to St Michael the Archangel for the use of the brothers serving God in the same place, St Michael near the Sea with all the appurtenances, namely vills, castles, lands and the rest, and adding also all the land of Vennesire (Winnington) with towns, vills, fields, meadows, lands cultivated and uncultivated with all their produce, moreover the port of Ruan Minor (Cadgewith) with the mills and fisheries and all things belonging to it,[1] we can hardly fail to recognise in Edward's grant of Vennesire (Winnington) the same lands as those held in his lifetime by the seventeen thegns, lands "which according to the testimony of the English had never paid geld",[2] and which were known as meneage or monastic lands.

"St Michael near the sea with all the appurtenances namely vills, castles, lands" doubtless includes the Mount and the Saint's demesne manor of Treiwal or Truthwall. This manor is described as never having paid the king's geld, but as having paid geld to St Michael.

It will be remembered that geld originated in the latter part of the tenth century in an attempt made by

---

[1] *Monasticon*, p. 31.
[2] Inquisitio Geldi.

King Ethelred II to buy off the repeated attacks of the Danes, and continued to be levied after the occasion for its imposition had ceased. If therefore the monastic lands in Cornwall had *never* paid geld they had been monastic long before Domesday Book was compiled. It would certainly appear from the considerations here put forward that both at the Mount and in the Meneage there had been powerful monastic influences at work long before the Confessor granted his charter. Whether they were already focussed at the Mount it is impossible to say. Edward the Confessor's charter may have had this very object in view. He was before all things a devout and earnest Churchman, and strongly attracted by the services of religion.

The question, however, immediately before us is whether by his charter, the contents of which have been given, he meant to convey the Mount with its possessions to Mont St Michel, or whether he meant by it to bestow Truthwall and the Meneage lands upon St Michael's Mount. Edward was a king of England, or rather, king of the English, and had no possessions in Normandy. Notwithstanding his affection and esteem for Norman ecclesiastics, upon whom he bestowed important offices, it is hardly likely that he intended to surrender to Normandy the Cornish Mount and its manors. The charter is entitled "Charter of Edward King of the English in favour of the *Abbey* of St Michael". But for its title, the charter would be equally applicable to the priory and the abbey of St Michael. When the Count of

Mortain had, with certain reservations, effected a transfer of the priory and lands to the abbey, soon afterwards, the registrar of the charters might be excused for entering both charters under the same head.

No mention is made of the religious order to which the monks at the Mount were to belong, that of St Benedict being the only form of the monastic life which was followed during the whole of the Saxon period in England.[1]

Reference has been made to Domesday Book, and the grant of King Edward has been equated with that of the Mount and the manor of Truthwall on the one hand and the lands held by seventeen thegns on the other. By William the Conqueror the Mount and all its possessions were bestowed upon Robert, Count of Mortain, his half-brother. It is not going beyond the truth to say that whenever we meet with a grant of lands by the count we recognise a deed of spoliation. He takes away two hides of St Michael's land in Truthwall and gives back one hide; he takes away the twenty-two manors held by seventeen thegns in Amaneth (Meneage) and gives back three (Cornish) acres. In this latter case there is no ambiguity or doubt as to which Mount is to benefit by his gift. By an undated charter to which the names of King William and his son, William Rufus, are appended as witnesses, he grants "St Michael's Mount (of) in Cornwall half a hide of land and a market on Thursday" and the above-mentioned lands to "St Michael

[1] Gasquet, *English Monastic Life in England*, p. 217.

(of) in Peril of the Sea"—the name by which the Norman Mount was then known. Normandy and England had become united by the Conquest, and it was no longer a question of surrendering English land to a foreign state. He gives these lands because he has more certainly recognised in the merits of Blessed Michael and in the prayers of the monks the grant by God of a son by his own wife (*ex propriâ conjuge meâ*). The lands specified are in Meneage and comprise Trevelaboth (Traboe), Lismanoch (Lesneage), Trequaners (Tregevas) and Carmailoc (Carvallack).

In the *Monasticon* there is appended to this charter what purports to be a confirmation of the grant by Bishop Leofric, who died in 1050!

The tenants, who before the Norman Conquest could not be separated from the manor, had given place to conventioners in the fifteenth century. The latter's holding was contractual; failing to perform their agreement, they were removable. Traboe, or the manor of Traboe, under which designation the tenements were known, embraced a water-mill at Cothas and the lands of Lesmanack, Polpurneck, Tregeg, Tregeg Wathan and Polker (in St Keverne), Trewathapp, Tregadras (in Mawgan), Tucoys (in Constantine), Carvelek (in St Martin), Carvellas, Trewellard and Gonhely. In 1482 the rents of these lands amounted to £16. 7s. 1d.

The next charter to be dealt with presents many difficulties. The Latin text will be found in the *Monasticon*, the original at Avranches. A translation

of it by Round, who assigns vaguely the date 1087–
91, is as follows:

Charter of Robert, Count of Mortain and Almodis his
wife. They give to St Michael and the monks of Luduhanam
(Ludgvan) a manor of Richard son of Turulf near the Mount
and the holding of Bloicus in the manor of Trevhalum
(Truthwall) and both of the fairs of the Mount. The Count
gives them to God and St Michael for the soul of William
King of the English and for the soul of King William his son
and for his own soul and that of his deceased wife Mathelda
and for his living wife one Almodis and for their boys. This
offering (*caritas*) is allowed by Robert his son, by the Countess
Almodis; and William his other son has promised to grant it if
Almodis should leave no heir and the lands should return to
him (i.e., William). In consideration of this grant Roger the
Abbot and his monks gave the Count £60 of the money of Le
Mans.[1]

Ten witnesses attest the charter. The names of
St Michael's are: Albertus monachus, Rainfredus de
Say monachus, Ligierius propositus, Guido de Monte
and Rogerus de Ardevone.

It is impossible to say whether the above grant is
in favour of the Norman or the Cornish Mount. The
name of Roger as Abbot of Mont St Michel does not
occur in the list of abbots as given by Oliver in his
Monasticon until the reign of Henry I, but in the sup-
plement he rightly calls attention to the fact that there
was another Roger who, as abbot in 1087, assisted at
the funeral of William the Conqueror. The two

[1] *Documents in France*, by J. H. Round, p. 256.

manors referred to in the charter, Truthwall and Ludgvan Leaze, held in 1086 respectively by Bloicus (Bluhid Brito) and Richard son of Turulf (Turold), remained in possession of them and their successors for centuries. If Roger the abbot gave the count £60 it seems certain that he got nothing in return. Moreover, it is difficult to see how the count could give that which was not his to give. He had stolen Truthwall from St Michael[1] in the first place and given it to Bloicus, and now proceeds to give it back to St Michael for £60. It will suffice to say that the charter was inoperative.

Before the middle of the twelfth century all questions of the Mount's status, rights and possessions had been placed on an accepted and solid basis. The church (*ecclesia*) of St Michael was a priory or cell of the abbey of Mont St Michel and to all sons of the Holy Church of God. Notification[2] was made that the church of St Michael of Cornwall was built by Bernard, Abbot of St Michel, in the year King Henry died (1135), and dedicated by Robert, Bishop of Exeter, in the ninth year of the reign of King Stephen at the prayer of the abbot there present. The abbot in his wisdom, by counsel of the bishop and with the approval of the Earl Ranulf[3] and the barons, arranged for thirteen brethren, making sufficient provision for their needs out of the previous endowments

[1] Domesday Book.
[2] This instrument is given in Oliver's *Monasticon*, p. 414, and in Round's *Documents in France*, p. 264.
[3] Ranulf was Reginald FitzHenry, Earl of Cornwall.

of the church and those given in his presence by the men of the province. He also appointed that the prior chosen by the Abbot of Mont St Michel should, in person or by one of his brethren, pay sixteen marks annually (to Mont St Michel). If he acted in contravention of this appointment, or set himself against the abbot and convent in anything, he was to be degraded from his office and replaced by one chosen by the abbot with the convent's advice. If he should be proud or contumacious and disobedient to the prelates of the Norman Mount he should lose all share in the benefits of that house, and be excommunicated by all churches in union with it. As to the brethren who might enter the community in Cornwall they should go to Mont St Michel to receive benediction as monks from the abbot, unless he happened to visit Cornwall and was willing to give it them there. Whoever should venture to infringe this ordinance, by diminishing the number of the monks or applying possessions of the house to other purposes, was to be sentenced to anathema.

The monks of Mont St Michel were of the Benedictine Order. Those of St Michael's Mount and of Tresco were also Benedictines. In the brief notices hereafter given of those who administered discipline at the Mount will be found little or nothing to suggest the learning and works of piety and charity for which the Order was distinguished. "The evil that men do lives after them, the good is oft interred with their bones." It may be that both at St Michael's Mount and also at Scilly we have a memento of their presence.

The Benedictines were gardeners. Dante alludes to this when speaking of

> Those other flames
> The spirits of men contemplative were all
> Enlivened by that warmth whose kindly force
> Gives birth to flowers and fruits of holiness.[1]

The narcissus known as the "Scilly White" is found indigenous at Mont St Michel, Scilly and St Michael's Mount, and may have been introduced to the two priories by monks from the abbey.

An addendum states that the possessions given to *St Michael of Cornwall* by Robert, Count of Mortain, are those already given in Count Robert's charter with the addition of Trevanne (? Tremain in St Martin) which had probably been included in one of the other holdings—in all twelve plough-lands. The notification is valuable because it clearly states that in 1135 Count Robert's grant was interpreted as having been made to St Michael's Mount.

The absolute supremacy of the Abbot of Mont St Michel in all matters connected with the priory of St Michael's Mount itself was, in practice, less prejudicial to the English king and Church than would appear at first sight. Normandy, at the time, was appendant to the English crown and the kings of England exercised more than their legitimate share in the appointment of the abbot. William the Conqueror, in spite of the opposition of the brethren of the abbey, appointed Ralph de Beaumont and, after

[1] *Paradiso*, XXII, 44.

Ralph's death, Roger, his own chaplain to be abbot. On the resignation of Roger, Henry I imposed upon the abbey Roger II and, after him, Richard de Mère, who wasted the resources of the abbey for personal profit and when summoned to appear before the papal legate retired from the office. Bernard du Bec, who succeeded him in 1131 and procured the erection and dedication of the priory of the Mount, owed his election to the abbacy to an agreement between Henry I and the monks of Mont St Michel. The choice was in every way excellent. Bernard set about reform and adopted an expedient which was at once unique, thorough and impartial. Every one who knows Mont St Michel knows its satellite Tombelaine, the barren sea-girt rock which lies about a mile and a half north-east of the Mont. There Abbot Bernard established a priory to consist of three monks and provided that, for their spiritual advantage, triads of the brethren belonging to the abbey should be sent there until the entire community had benefited by the discipline. Bernard was not only a reformer; he was like many of his predecessors, an architect and builder. Mont St Michel owed to him its clock-tower at the intersection of the choir and transepts. He enriched the windows of the nave with stained glass, some portions of which were discovered in 1875. The discipline administered by him, harsh as it may seem, was mild as compared with that to which refractory monks were sometimes subjected. At Mont St Michel, for example, there were "*in pace* cells" in which groaned from time to time monks who had been guilty of disobedience. There were cases where the motive for seeking admission to a monastery was an unworthy one and revolt against the ruler of the Order required and received punishment. It is possible that the dungeon at St Michael's Mount served some such purpose.

Somewhere about this time—the *Cartulary* gives the date as 1140 but the Charter Roll omits it— Matilda, Countess of Meulan (*Mellento*), daughter of Reginald, Earl of Cornwall, whose name appears as Ranulf in the last-cited document, gave

to St Michael of Cornwall and the monks there serving God, for the weal of her soul and those of her predecessors all the land of Lambessow (Lambedou) with all its appurtenances and the land which the monks previously held of her in the vill of Moresk (Moreis) by St Clement's well and de Gimas and the land of David the chamberlain, with all their appurtenances quit of all secular dues and service for ever. The monks and their tenants in these lands are to have such common rights as her own tenants, in wood and plain, pasture lands and elsewhere.

This benefaction became an important source of income to the monks and was followed in 1205 by a grant of two advowsons, as appears from a charter of Henry, Bishop of Exeter, in the following terms:

He grants out of charity to the *Abbey of Mont St Michel* and the monks there serving God, for defraying the reception of pilgrims and guests the following churches in his diocese, at their first vacancy, to be devoted to their own uses in alms for ever....St Clement (Morris) and St Hilary, saving an honourable provision for the chaplains serving the churches, who shall be responsible to him and his successors for the bishop's rights and saving in all things the rights of himself and his successors.

Whether the Abbot of Mont St Michel ever administered the patronage of the churches of St Clement and St Hilary we have been unable to discover. It is certain that it was the prior and not the abbot who presented in 1329 to St Clement, in 1343 to St Hilary, and continued to do so until the dissolution of the priory except at such times when England was at war with France, when the king took into his hands the patronage of all alien priories.

A charter of very great interest dated 1140 will be found in the *Cartulary*, the *Monasticon* and Round's *Documents*. It relates to dues amounting to ten shillings derivable from a fair at Medresem which Alan, Count of Brittany, Earl of Cornwall and Richmond, grants to the church of St Michael's Mount in the Sea, for the health of the souls of himself, his wife and children, for the salvation (*redemptione*) of the soul of Brient his uncle, of whose inheritance he possesses land in Cornwall, for the salvation of his ancestors and parents and for the stability of my lord King Stephen, his children and wife. The witnesses to this transaction, happily completed (*feliciter peracta*) at Bomne (Bodmin), include Conan his chaplain, Richard de Luci, Racor de Valle Torta and others.

Alan's uncle Brient, in 1086, held considerable lands in Cornwall. He was the son of Eudo, Count of Penthièvre, and brother of Stephen of Brittany and of Alan le Roux. The last named became Earl of Richmond. The grantor of the fair was Alan le Noir, second son of Stephen, and his wife was Bertha, daughter of Duke Conan III. Had he lived, Alan le Noir would have become Duke of Brittany. He had already received the Earldom of Cornwall in 1140 and had inherited that of Richmond from Alan le Roux.

Richard, Earl of Cornwall, confirmed Alan's grant in 1301 and stated that the fair was in the hands of William de Walebraus (Whalesborough) who had paid ten shillings yearly for the *fair of St James*. The Whalesborough family had acquired the manor of Uthno before 1213 when, on the death of Pharam de Whalesborough, his widow Osemund was granted one-third of his lands in dower. It would be interesting if it could be shown that the family was descended from Bristric who held the manor of Uthno at the time of the Domesday Survey. The fact that the Whalesboroughs held Uthno in chief lends colour to this suggestion.

The fair of St James was held at Goldsithney and continues to be held there on August 5th, like that of Jacobstow, on St James's day (old style).

There can be little doubt that long before we have documentary evidence of it the port of the Mount and its emporium on the mainland—Marazion— had an importance shared by no other sea port in West Cornwall. Penzance became a port some centuries later. Mousehole and Fowey were probably the only ports on the south coast which could claim to rival it in point of antiquity, and Mousehole was never of much consequence. Before and after the Norman Conquest the port and market of the Mount were widely known.

One of the most entertaining episodes in the romance of *Tristan and Iseult*, which assumed literary form probably towards the end of the eleventh century, is connected with the Mount. When the two lovers, during their escapade in the forest of Moresk, which at that time extended from the Fal to the Helford river, had met the hermit Ogrin and had been advised by him; and Iseult had resolved to return to her husband, King Mark, Ogrin was sent to the Mount to procure a fresh outfit for the queen. We are told that he bought in plenty, silks, green and grey and purple-brown, clothes of fine wool and white linen whiter than the lily flower, and a sweetly ambling palfrey caparisoned in shining gold. Still he went on buying, brocades and furs both grey and ermined such as may splendidly adorn the queen.

> Li hermites en vet au Mont,
> Por les recheces qui la sont
> Assés achate ver et gris
> Dras de soie et de porpre bis
> Escarlates et blanc chainsil
> Auz plus blanc que flor de lil,
> Et palefroi souef anblant
> Bien atorné d'or flanboiant.
> Ogrins l'ermite tant achate
> Et tant accroit et tant barate.
> Pailes, vairs et gris et hermine
> Qui richement vest la roine.

When she arrived at the court of King Mark, we are told that from her neck she removed her cape of costly wool, and wore a tunic, and underneath a flowing costume of silk. And what shall be said of her mantle? The hermit who bought it regretted not the price. Rich in robe and elegant in person, her eyes sparkled and her hair rippled.

> Du col li a osté la chape
> Qui ert d'escarlate mot riche
> Ele out vestu une tunique
> Desus un grant blaiut de soie.
> De son mantel que vos diroie?
> Ains l'ermite qui l'achata
> Le riche fuer ne regreta.
> Riche ert la robe et gent le cors,
> Les eulz ont vers, les cheveus sors.

At the time when the romance came to be written, Celtic, Saxon and Norman were spoken languages in Cornwall. No other province could claim this distinction. On linguistic grounds alone, apart from the place-names which occur in the romance and have been identified with places in the county, Professor Loth has shown that its provenance, in the form in which we have it, could only have been Cornwall and that the two Iseults represent a juxtaposition of the Cornish and Breton legends. It is hardly likely that the romance would appeal to the Saxon element which had held Cornwall in subjection for a couple of centuries but which was now deprived of its supremacy and dispossessed of its lands. The affinity of

Breton and Norman was considerably stronger than that between Briton and Saxon. Many Bretons, who spoke the same language as the Cornish, assisted King William in his conquest of England and received from him a rich reward: among them may be mentioned Blohiu (Bloyou), Jovin, Brient, Richard son of Turold and Judhael. To these and their descendants, equally with the native Cornish, the romance would bring back

> Those shadowy recollections,
>   Which be they what they may,
> Are yet the fountain light of all our day.

recollections of the wonderful days when Arthur and his knights fought the rude invader of their land, when, all of one blood, they were bonded together against a common foe. Very precious to every true-hearted man is the recollection of the past, and perhaps no rôle was ever more fitted for a broken soldier like the younger Winslade than when, stripped of all his worldly possessions, with harp and companion, he wandered from house to house singing in his mother tongue the strange adventures of Tristan and Iseult.

It is by no means improbable that some of the first to welcome the setting of the story, as it appeared in the eleventh century, were those magnates whose names have been given.

Be that as it may, the poet tells us that it was to the Mount that the hermit Ogrin directed his steps, when he was commissioned to buy gay clothing for Queen Iseult. Its markets were known far and wide. Here it is proposed to attempt the disentangling of the mass of material concerning them. Two cautions are needed. The task is not an easy one, and it must not be supposed that the grant of a market excludes the possibility of its being already in existence. Quite the contrary. A market exists before you can give or sell the dues which accrue from it. Domesday Book, which records only one market in Devonshire, records six in Cornwall. Of these six, three had been seized by the Count of Mortain, and one had been rendered worthless by the count who had set up another near it. It would, therefore, be unsafe to conclude that Domesday Book gives a complete list of the markets in Devon and Cornwall.

We have seen that Count Robert granted to Mont St Michel a market to be held on Thursdays (*feria quinta*) and half a hide of land near the Mount. This would be at Marketjew[1] in that portion of the manor of Truthwall probably which he had taken from St Michael of Cornwall. In the second charter he and his wife Almodis granted two fairs, belonging to the Mount, to Mont St Michel. Mention has been already made of Count Alan's grant in 1140 of the profits of a fair at Medresem to St Michael's Mount in the Sea. About this time St Michael's Mount became a recognised priory of the abbey of St Michel, the only render to the Norman house being an apport of sixteen marks yearly. There is no longer any doubt as to the identity of St Michael. The Cornish Mount is free to receive whatever gifts may be offered, and

[1] Marketjew = "Marghas yew", the Thursday market.

the abbot has to be content with his yearly apport. The benefactions which in earlier charters have been described as having been bestowed upon Mont St Michel are now regarded as gifts to the Cornish priory. Towards the end of the eleventh century Richard, King of the Romans, by charter[1] confirmed to the Prior of St Michael's Mount *in Cornwall* three fairs and three markets, namely, on the day and morrow of mid-Lent, the eve, day and morrow of Michaelmas and the eve, day and morrow of St Michael in Monte Tumba (May 8th), which, *by grant of his predecessors*, had hitherto been held on others' land at Marghas bigan (Marazion), to be held on their own land at Marcadyou (Marketjew). Also Henry de Heligan, Lord of Brevannic,[2] who had been for a long time a thorn in the side of the prior, quit-claimed to him all the customs derived from his fairs both before and after laying down the glove.[3] And finally, as the result of an enquiry held by Sir John de Berewyk, the chief justice of the Cornish iter, confirmed to him his right to the assize of "bread and ale".

The favour shown to the prior by Richard and Edmund led to reprisals on the part of the Lord of Truthwall, who held in demesne the lands bestowed by the Conqueror upon Blohiu. In 1331 Ralph Bloyou obtained for himself and his heirs a market on Monday at Marghesyon (Marazion) and a fair there

---

[1] *Cartulary* at Hatfield.
[2] Brevannick was situated west of the old vicarage in Marazion.
[3] *Cartulary* at Hatfield.

on the eve, day and morrow of St Andrew (November 30th), but, apparently, to little purpose.

After the suppression of the abbey of Syon the whole of its possessions, including the Mount with its lands, fairs and markets, were confiscated.

In 1595 Queen Elizabeth granted to Marazion a charter of incorporation to consist of a mayor, eight aldermen and twelve capital burgesses, and, ratifying St Andrew's fair, granted another on the feast of St Barnabas (June 11th) and a market on Saturday. Under the Municipal Corporations Act the municipality was dissolved and the property belonging to it vested in charity commissioners. All the markets are gone and only the prior's Michaelmas fair and that at Goldsithney survive.

Another valuable source of revenue was the tithe of certain lands. The origin of some of it is not difficult to trace as, for example, that of St Clement and St Hilary, which had passed to the prior along with the advowsons. As regards the rest we are left to conjecture. Complaints were frequent. The prior's claims were opposed. In 1364 the Bishop of Exeter ordered a visitation of the Archdeaconry of Cornwall and appointed visitors under his official seal. The visitors chosen were William Carslak, Adam Spark and Simon Withial, canons of the collegiate church of St Thomas the Martyr, Glasney. In the following year they duly reported as follows:

Know ye that we duly visited the deanery of Penwith, where we found that Brother John Voland, monk of the order of

St Benedict, Prior of St Michael, had received and was receiving (so it was said) contrary to the provisions of the
canons, two-thirds of the tithes, as well the greater as the less,
out of two-thirds of the manor of Alverton in the parish of
St Madern and two-thirds of the greater tithes of the manor of
Tehidy in the parish of St Illogan and also from the lordship
of Reskagel in the parish of Cambron. We summoned the
said prior to shew by what title he did this. He appeared before us by his proctor, Master Richard Trenemyny, whose
letters of proxy bore the seal of the dean of Penwith. He produced divers muniments showing the Prior's right and a sum-
mary petition supported by the evidence of divers witnesses.
After examination thereof we made a definitive sentence by
common consent, certifying that the Prior had proved his
title to the aforesaid tithes to our satisfaction in the chapel of
St Mary Penryn 10th July, 1365, in the presence of John
Reda and Stephen Dauwa, clerks of the diocese of Exeter.

The visitors also inspected, at the personal request
of the prior, a certificate concerning the churches of
St Hilary and St Clement of Moresk, which the prior
held in appropriation to which the seal of the Deanery
of Penwith had been appended at Marghasion on the
Wednesday next after the Feast of the Translation of
St Thomas the Martyr, 1362.

The origin of the Alverton tithe payable to the
prior appears to have been a grant made by Lord
Tyes who held half of the manor of Alverton by
grant of Richard, King of the Romans, by the render
to the Earl of Cornwall yearly at Michaelmas of one
ebony bow without a cord and three barbed arrows.
After the death of the second Lord Tyes, who had

joined the Earl of Lancaster in his rebellion against Edward II and shared his fate, it was found by inquisition that *inter alia* he held a capital messuage and a chapel and that service was held daily in the chapel by the Prior of St Michael and by the rector of the church of St Maddern, and that mass was celebrated in it three days a week. This was the chapel of Our Lady at Penzance described in the chantry roll as "dystante from the parishe churche ii myles and a halff, founded by Syr Henry Tyes Knt., lord of the mannor of Alverton who gave iiii^{ly} owt of the lands of the sayd manor for the salarye of a prest to celebrate there".[1] It was, accordingly, suppressed by the Chantry Acts and its tithe confiscated.

Yet another source of revenue was the tithe of fish. For its origin we must go back to the time when tithe was personal rather than predial, when every member of the Church, as such, was under the obligation to devote one-tenth of his income to God. When a church or a monastery furnished the boats and quay the obligation was enhanced, and eventually became a condition of being allowed to fish. It would be interesting to discover whether fishery tithe was one of the characteristics of Celtic Christianity. We are not dealing with fishery rights but with the tithe of fish. It is found in Wales and Cornwall. Did it exist in Brittany? An answer in the affirmative would carry us back to the emigration of Britons to Armorica in the fifth and sixth centuries. In Cornwall, Padstow paid fishery tithe to the Prior of Bodmin; Lelant to

[1] Oliver, *Monasticon*, p. 490.

the collegiate church of Crediton; St Just in Penwith to the vicar. It is fortunate that the Easter Book of the last-named parish for the years 1588 to 1596 has been preserved and furnishes the ancient rules in this connection. The rules are (1) that fishermen "whenas they come to land to divide their shares, shall first take out the tithe fish, leaving it in the same place, the vicar or his deputy to give their attendance without any warning. (2) Att Easter a man that useth to feshe at the Rock or Stone commonly is to pay iid at Easter to the vicar or his depute and no more". The rock referred to is at Ayr Point and is still used for fishing from the shore, but fish tithe has long ceased to be paid.

The fishery tithe of St Michael's Mount is mentioned in the Taxatio of St Hilary made by Bishop Bronescombe in the year 1261 which reserves to the prior its fishery tithe (*ex batellis parochianorum*) and all tithes of St Michael's Mount. In the Compotus roll of 1482 the tithe of fish forms a not inconsiderable item. The tithe of ling amounted to 12s. 10d. and of dried dentrics (*dentric arid*) to £9. The latter— whether hake or pilchard—was for exportation.[1] When in the year 1427 the king, at the instance of William Morton, chaplain of the Mount, consented to assist in providing a better haven for ships there, he was authorised to levy a fine of 12d. upon every strange boat fishing in the bay for the fish called hake or hake of that value. Tithe of fish continued to be

[1] It is possible that dentric is the name of the port to which the fish was taken. Some of the ling is described as Mylwell.

paid after the suppression of the religious house. In 1631 William, Earl of Salisbury, granted to Hannibal Newman the tithe of fish belonging to the Mount and the cellar used for curing the same except the tithe fish of Porthenals, for four years at £20 a year.

The Priors

IN the Notification[1] of 1135 the Abbot of Mont
St Michel reserves to himself the right of appoint-
ing the Prior of St Michael's Mount. No record
has been preserved of ecclesiastical appointments
made in Devon and Cornwall prior to the episcopate
of Bishop Bronescombe who, in 1258, succeeded
Richard Blondy in the See of Exeter. In 1266 the
abbot appointed *Ralph de Cartaret* to be prior and he
was duly instituted[2] by Bishop Bronescombe on
December 21st of that year. Upon his death or
cession there appears to have been some delay on the
part of the abbot to fill the vacancy. The right of
presentation fell to the bishop, who in 1276 collated
Fr. Richard Perer, a monk of St Michael in Periculo
Maris (the Norman Mount).

Richard Perer was succeeded in 1283 by *Galfrid de
Gerenon* alias *Forum* who, in 1287, with the consent
of his fellow monks, but to the impoverishment of the
priory, granted to Michael de Tremenhir Woles, for
services and various friendly acts done to the priory,
half a (Cornish) acre of land in Tremenhir Woles.[3]
Eight years later the same Michael received from
Stephen de Beaupré two-thirds of half a Cornish acre in
Tremenhir Wartha, which Stephen held of the prior.

Galfrid de Gerenon resigned in 1316 and was suc-

---

[1] See p. 35.
[2] *Exeter Episcopal Registers, Bronescombe*, p. 175.
[3] See *The Tremenheres*, by S. G. Tremenhere, pp. 13, 14.

ceeded as prior by *Peter de Cara Villa*, otherwise *Carvill*.

For some time prior to Carvill's appointment there had been a struggle between the Bishop of Exeter and the king respecting the bishop's rights as ordinary of St Buryan. The bishop had to contend not only with his sovereign, but also with certain persons of that parish who had taken advantage of the quarrel to create disturbance and to refuse payment of tithe. In fact there had been a free fight and bloodshed within the precincts of the church itself. The circumstances are fully reported in the Episcopal Registers. On November 4th, 1328, the bishop in person at St Michael's Mount attended by Richard Beaupré, Rector of St Just in Penwith, whom the bishop had appointed to a canonry of St Buryan, with his lordship's two chaplains and an Augustinian canon of Lanthony wearing stoles and bearing candles, pronounced the Greater Excommunication against John Kaer, who though excommunicate himself "was celebrating or rather profaning" in an unconsecrated and forbidden place; against Richard Penrose otherwise excommunicate who had usurped the bishop's jurisdiction; against Richard Vyvyan the patron and promoter of many evils; against all those and all who supported them; and against those who had laid violent hands on Richard Beaupré! Also he interdicted the church and churchyard polluted by the effusion of blood. Finally as the candles were extinguished he pronounced the sentence, *Sicut ista luminaria...extinguuntur...animae extinguantur*, with the saving clause, "unless they repent and come to their senses" (*nisi peniteant et resipiscant; fiat fiat*).

During Carvill's priorship Bishop Grandisson commissioned his chancellor, Richard de Wideslade, to enquire into the truth of a report that he was dissipating the goods of the priory. The chancellor reported in 1336 that the income of the priory was £100 besides the oblations, that there was a debt of £5 owing to various creditors, that the prior had farmed (i.e. let) the lands to persons for a miserable rent and sold corn to those from whom he could not expect the full price. There was, moreover, a relative of his, who was wasting the goods of the priory, whom neither he nor the monks would name and the prior had, contrary to the monastic rule, stayed alone in the priory for over a month. Also he had failed to produce evidence of the priory's right to advowsons which he asserted had been appropriated to it.[1]

In the following year, 1337, in view of the war impending between England and France, the king seized into his own hands all alien priories and caused a survey to be made of all their lands, benefices and goods. William de Hardeshull, clerk, and John Hamely of the county were appointed for this purpose in Cornwall. They found in the priory of St Michael's Mount the following goods:[2]

---

[1] *Exeter Episcopal Registers, Grandisson*, 1336.
[2] The inventory will be found in the *Monasticon*, p. 29. The above translation is that of the late Mr Thurstan C. Peter which may be compared with that of Sir E. Smirke (*Journ. Roy. Inst. of Cornwall*, 11).

Goods and chattels found in the priory of St Michael's Mount. In the church a chalice of the weight of 20s. 10d. sterling. Item, a vestment with two lappets of silk worth 26s. 8d. Item, a missal worth 13s. 4d. Item, in the custody of the Prior and monks, two worn cloths (*vestes*) with six towels worth 20s. Item, a chalice of the weight of 16s. 1d. Item, one worn clerk's breviary (*portiforium*) worth 6s. 8d. These were left to the custody of the priory under supervision of the Sheriff. Item, in the Prior's chamber three lavers and one ewer (*pelves cum lavatorio*) worth 3s. 6d. Item, four chests with a coffer (*forcerio*) worth 6s. 8d. Item, eight silver spoons weighing 8s. 4d. Item, two wooden cups (*ciphi de mazero*) worth 10s. Item, a silver cup, with cover of the same, weighing 20s. 10d. Item, a silver cup weighing 18s. 4d. Item, a silver cup, with cover, weighing 31s. 8d. Item, broken silver weighing 4s. 6d. Item, a certain silver image weighing 11½d. Item, a silver buckle (*firmaculum*) weighing 6d. Item, an image of St Michael worth 13s. 4d.[1] Item, two cups of wood, old and broken, worth 5s. Item, one silver thurible weighing 35s. 8d. Item, one silver thurible weighing 21s. Item, five small and old tin vases (or mugs) (*olle de stagno*) worth 12d. Item, four brass vases (*olle encae*) worth 6s. 8d. Item, worn pans (*patelle*) worth 2s. Item, fifteen plates (*disci*) and fifteen worn saucers (*salsaria*) worth 15d. Item, one bowl and other iron utensils worth 23d. Item, in store three heifers (*afferi*) worth 10s.! Item, wooden vessels worth 6s. 8d. Item, the tithes of the church of Moresk are taxed at £15. Item, the tithes of the church of St Hilary with the tithe of the chapel of St Michael £23. 6s. 8d. Item, the

[1] In the above the reader can easily reduce the value of the silver articles to weight troy when he remembers that twenty silver pennies equal one ounce.

Prior's rents from the Vill of Treverabo with its appurtenances £22. Item, the said Prior's rents from Penwith 29s. 7½d. Item, the tithe of the fishery at this place and the varying casual oblations which remain in the custody of the Sheriff to account for (?£4. 13s. 3d.). Total £82. 3s. 11d.

The seizure of the goods of alien priories was merely a precaution. When peace was concluded they were restored to the priors as a matter of course.

In 1342 Peter Carvill was succeeded by *Nicholas Isabel*. Together with others, including some persons of note, he was charged in the following year with having taken prises belonging to Edward, Earl of Cornwall, presumably at St Michael's Mount. Nothing came of the charge. In 1348 he made a grant of lands to Richard de Trenemyny, clerk, and Richard, son of John de Trewartharap, and the grant was confirmed by letters patent.[1] The lands are described as messuages and lands with appurtenances in Tregemyny, Polker and Breglos, to wit, those which Richard held already of the gift of the present prior and those which John le Tagy lately held in Tregemyny, together with those held by the said Richard of the gift of Peter Carvill, late prior. The lands were to be held by either of them for life and for one year more along with common of pasture in the prior's moor of Gohenhely (Goonhilly Downs) for all manner of animals, and estovers of peat and other fuel in the moor at a yearly rent, for the first

[1] Letters Pat. 12, June, 1348, p. 107. Chan. Inq. p.m. 10 Richard II, p. 109.

twenty years of eight shillings and twelve capons at St Andrew, mid-Lent, St James the Apostle and Michaelmas for all service save suit of court at the manor of Trewarabo (Traboe) and the accustomed suit of the mill and three days' work and the render, at the end of twenty years, of forty-eight shillings and twelve capons as above.

On the death of Richard de Trenemyny in 1386 it was found that Richard had held the above-mentioned lands, described as Trenemyny, Power and Breglos, and letters patent were issued in the same year to Richard, son of John de Trewartherap, on the same terms.

The war with France was not conducive to the prior's peace of mind. During the priorship of Peter Carvill a summons to appear before the king and council was of frequent occurrence, and there was no abatement of the interruption when he had been succeeded by Nicholas Isabel. As already stated, the revenue and patronage of the Mount and its possessions fell to the king in time of war. In 1345, the vicarage of St Hilary being vacant, the king appointed William de Alesby. In February of the following year, rumours of discontent having reached the council, that certain persons were prosecuting appeals to the court of Rome in derogation of the king's presentation, a commission consisting of the Sheriff of Cornwall and Oger de Kernyk was appointed to enquire and to take all those indicted by such inquisition and have them before the king and council a fortnight after Easter. The enquiry was apparently fruitless, for we find that in the following November protection was granted to the prior and to Master Stephen Pempel for two years in order that they might render the accounts of the farm of the priory's lands and possessions more promptly.[1]

John Hardy succeeded Nicholas Isabel in 1349. Seven years later he was indicted at Launceston on a charge of having sent secret letters, two years before, with a sum in gold and silver amounting to £60 into Normandy to the king's enemies, and of having harboured two men from that country for two weeks at Trevaberou (Traboe). He proved his innocence and was acquitted.[2]

On his death, in 1362, *John de Volant* was admitted prior. During his term of office a survey was made of the priory, and it was found that he and two monks only were in residence at the Mount, that it was valued at twenty-four marks, three shillings and nine pence yearly, and that St Hilary and Moresk were appendant and rendered respectively five and a half marks and twenty marks, six shillings and sixpence to the priory.

The date of John de Volant's cession or death is not known. There was a delay in filling the vacancy. The priory was in the king's hands.

It was about this time that a horrible crime was committed at Trevarthian in St Hilary, of which particulars are recorded in the Episcopal Register.[3] On September 14th, 1380, the bishop ordered the

---

[1] Pat. Rolls, 20 Edward III, Nov. 20th.
[2] Pat. Rolls, 30 Edward III, quoted by Dr Oliver.
[3] *Exeter Episcopal Registers, Brantyngham*, pp. 156, 434, 438.

archdeacons together with the Rectors of St Stephen's
in Brannel and Camborne to investigate the truth of a
report which had reached him of the murder in Cornwall of a priest by some person or persons unknown,
and to report to him. In the following October the
bishop issued a mandate to the archdeacons and
clergy of their archdeaconries to pronounce the
Greater Excommunication, with book, bell and
candle against one John Browdrer, who described
himself as a serjeant-at-arms of the king, and his
accomplices, for the murder of a priest, Master
William Sancre at Trevarthian, by violently seizing
him, tying his hands behind his back and cutting off
his head with a sword and afterwards carrying it
away publicly on a spear to London, as if the priest
had been an abominable traitor, albeit common report described him as a man of good reputation and
blameless life. On November 18th following the
bishop ordered the Greater Excommunication to be
pronounced against Roger Trewinnard, one of
Browdrer's accomplices, stating that Roger's complicity was so notorious that by no sort of subterfuge
could it be concealed. We are not informed of the
cause of the priest's murder. Roger Trewinnard was
the head of an ancient St Erth family which had derived its name from a manor in that parish, a name
known to students of constitutional history owing to
the arrest for debt of William Trewinnard in 1543.
William Trewinnard[1] had been returned Member of

[1] Nicholas Hals, the fertility of whose imagination was amazing,
has given us a lurid description (*Parochial History of Cornwall*, I,

Parliament for Helston the previous year, and was consequently exempt from arrest and imprisonment during its session.[1]

It should also be needless to remark that Roger's excommunication is no proof of his guilt, but a challenge to him to prove his innocence. Whether he did so is not known, but in 1405 the wardship of his sons Henry and James, who were minors, was granted to John Boscawen. They must, therefore, have been born more than five years after the sentence of excommunication was pronounced.

The priory being vacant, in 1383 the king's escheator in Cornwall appears to have taken the matter into his own hands and to have presented Richard Harepath, an Augustinian canon regular of St Germans, to the vacant benefice. St Michael's Mount was a Benedictine monastery. It is possible that it was this irregularity which moved the bishop to look into the matter. However this may be, on June 15th, 1383, he addressed a letter to the official of his peculiar jurisdiction and the Vicars of Bodmin

357) of Deiphobus Trewinnard, the last male representative of the family, who in his rage killed an innocent man and buried his body in the chapel at Trewinnard for which he was arrested and committed to the assizes at Launceston, where he was condemned to be hanged. Sir Reginald Mohun, however, a favourite of Queen Elizabeth, procured his pardon from the queen, which arrived at the last moment and saved his life. The story is, like many others of the same author, a pure fabrication.

[1] For an account of Trewinnard's case and its implications, see Prynne, *Reg. of Parl. Writs*, and Courtney, *Parliamentary History of Cornwall*.

and St Hilary in which he states that one Richard
Harepath, by virtue of certain letters wrongly forged
(*falso modo fabricatarum*) by the escheator in the king's
name, has made himself Prior of St Michael's Mount,
and by force and arms has done his best to enter the
priory, and the bishop, under pain of the Greater Excommunication, commands the above-named to refuse to institute the said Richard and cites all three,
together with the archdeacon, to appear before him
on the following Feast of St Peter ad Vincula.[1]
Richard Harepath, though foiled in his attempt to
obtain the priory of St Michael's Mount, was nevertheless successful in obtaining that of St Germans. In
1385 the Bishop notifies the Rural Dean of East and
the Vicar of Landrake that the priory of St Germans
is vacant by the resignation of William Treskelli, and
that the brothers have chosen Richard Harepath. The
rural dean is to cause proclamation of this to be made
in the church of the convent of St Germans that, if
any objection is brought forward, he must cite the
objectors to appear before him or his commissary at
his manor of Chudleigh.

In the same year, 1385, the king presented *Richard
Auncell*, a monk of the abbey of Tavistock, to St
Michael's Priory, which was in his gift on account of
the war with France and, in the following year, ap-
pointed a commission consisting of John Kentwode,
John Aston, escheator in Cornwall, and the Sheriff of
Cornwall to enquire touching the waste and dilapida-
tion of the priory whilst it was in the king's hands and

[1] *Exeter Episcopal Registers, Brantyngham*, p. 497.

what goods and chattels remained therein and their value. This was doubtless in consequence of the surrender of the priory into the king's hands in or before 1383, when Letters Patent had been revoked by which the Mount had been granted to John Penlyn, chaplain, and John Rose, the king's servitor. The reason assigned for the revocation of the grant to Penlyn and Rose is stated to be a grant of the same to the king's mother in dower and the prior's life interest in it. On that account the prior was to have the custody of it in preference to others. In spite of Prior Auncell's appointment by the king he found that his position was by no means secure. Dr Oliver[1] gives a long list of the repressive measures extending over a period of 170 years aimed by the king and parliament against alien priories. Richard II had showed them little favour. Auncell had been removed. Henry IV, on his accession, sought the good will of the clergy and Auncell was restored. As explained elsewhere a distinction was made between those alien priories which were conventual and those which were dependent upon a foreign abbey.

Auncell had been removed on the ground that his priory was not conventual. He had rightly maintained that it *was*, but in spite of his protest before the council, the Bishop of St David's, then treasurer, had compelled him to take it to farm at an annual payment of £20. In 1399 the priory was restored to him on condition that he paid the apport (of sixteen

[1] *Monasticon*, p. 425.

marks), during the war with France, not to the abbot but to the king, that he supported the monks and paid the tenths and other subsidies granted by the clergy and commonalty. This provision was somewhat modified in 1403. Instead of the apport of sixteen marks he was required to pay £10 yearly to the king during the war with France. During his priorship, in 1395 to be exact, the Abbot of Mont St Michel petitioned the king that, inasmuch as he had various priories, founded by the king's predecessors in the king's dominions, and that to all of them, save St Michael's Mount and Lay, in Jersey, he had appointed such persons to govern them as he had pleased, he prayed the king that he might have the same privilege in the case of the excepted priories. This petition the king granted provided that the appointee of the abbot must be an adherent of Pope Boniface IX and of good behaviour to the king and people.[1] At this time the anti-pope was Clement VII who resided at Avignon. Prior Auncell died in the year 1410. Dr Oliver, writing in 1846, states that his brass seal, St Michael transfixing the dragon, "was not long since discovered at Exeter and is now at Prior Park near Bath".

Richard Auncell's successor was *William Lambert*, a monk of Tutbury in Staffordshire. He was admitted by Bishop Stafford on October 21st, 1412, on the presentation of King Henry IV. In the two years following, Acts of Parliament were passed under

[1] Pat. Rolls, 1395, Sept. 26th.

which all the possessions of alien monasteries were vested in the crown except those which were conventual and whose priors were instituted and inducted. Under these Acts St Michael's Mount was entitled to exemption. Henry V thought otherwise. The first intimation of the king's intentions is contained in a letter written in 1421 by Simon Teravo, nuncio and papal collector of procurations, to the Bishop of Exeter's vicar-general in which he states that he has learnt that the priories of Otterton and St Michael's Mount have been appropriated to the house of Schune (Sheen) during the papacy of the present pope (*tempore papae moderni*). This would be Martin V, who reigned from 1417 to 1431. The appropriation must therefore have taken place between 1417 and 1421. In a mandate addressed by the bishop to his clergy in 1421 the *Prior* of St Michael's Mount is included, but in 1425, in summoning the clergy to a synod, the *Clergy* of the Mount are included. This fixes Lambert's death or resignation between 1421 and 1425. A Patent Roll of 1424,[1] that is, three years after the death of King Henry V, may be quoted in this connection.

King Henry V proposing to found a certain house of religious persons in his manor of Istelworth in the county of Middlesex, granted to Thomas, bishop of Durham and Edmund then bishop of Hereford, Thomas Duke of Exeter, Henry Fitz Hugh, knight, Roger Flore and other persons since deceased, a plot of land out of the demesne of his manor

[1] Pat. Rolls, 2 Henry VI, Oct. 20th.

of Istelworth in the parish of Twykenham in the said county
with the buildings thereon, the priory of Oterton, the priory
of St Michael's Mount in the county of Cornwall [and various
lands and reversions etc., in various parts of England]. Thomas
bishop of Durham and others being seised of certain lands pro-
pose, in accordance with the will of Henry V, to grant them in
frankalmoin to the Abbess and Convent of the Holy Saviour
and of SS. Mary the Virgin and Bridget of Syon of the
Augustinian order but have not yet obtained licence; now
therefore the King, by the advice of the lords spiritual and
temporal and of the commonalty of the realm, confirms the
said letters patent.

The Bishop of Exeter was himself at St Michael's
Mount on April 17th, 1425, doubtless in order to
arrange for its future welfare. As a priory it no
longer existed, but the bishop determined that it
should continue to serve its original purpose as a
church. Of late there had been only three monks in
residence, and he decided that it should have three
chaplains, the chief of whom should be styled archpriest. It has been stated that the title of archpriest is
only found in one instance applied to the senior
chaplain. On the contrary William Morton in a
Compotus Roll of 1432, Ralph Crabbe in a similar roll
of 1482, and John Arscott, in a dispensation granted
in 1537 by Archbishop Cranmer, are all styled
archpriests. The title signifies nothing more than the
chief or senior priest or chaplain in charge.

It is fortunate that the indenture by which the
Abbess of Syon committed the church and its orna-

ments to the archpriest, William Morton, should have been preserved.[1] It reads as follows:

This Indenture made between Johanna Abbess of the Monastery of our Saviour and Saints Marie the virgin and Brigette of Syon, of the order of Saint Augustine of the Saviour, and the convent of the same place and solemnly declared of the one part; and William Morton, Archpriest of the Mount of Saint Michael, of the other part, Witnesseth.

That the aforesaid Abbess and Convent on the first day of October in the ninth year of Henry the sixth after the conquest (1430) delivered to the aforesaid William various goods and chattels and other things below written belonging to the Church and Chapel and Priory of Mount St Michael in the County of Cornwall, namely:

TRANSLATION

Firstly. In the Church of Saint Michael. Two Chests. Two Chalices parcel gilt, and two Chalices of silver, a Tabernacle of silver parcel gilt with a birrell appointed for carrying the body of Christ at processions.

Item. An image of Saint Michael on the dragon, on a silver foot wholly gilt.

Item. A pix of silver parcel gilt with its canopy of silk over it to protect the body of Christ hanging before the Altar.

Item. Two silver cruets for wine and water for the service of the Mass.

Item. A silver Thurible; one pax of silver called "paxbreyde".

---

[1] The copy was made by the late Mr Michell Whitley and will be found in *Devon and Cornwall Notes and Queries* for April 1915. It is here printed by permission.

Item. Two Missals of the use of Sarum. Two Breviaries Sarum. A gradual of the use of Sarum. A Processional of the use of Sarum. A Legend book of the use of Sarum. Another Legend book of the use of Sarum.

Item. Two Missals for the use of the Monks.

Item. A gradual for the use of the Monks.

Item. A complete set of vestments of white silk called "damaske"; with a set of frontals for the altar of Saint Michael with two angels and the Crucifixion embroidered on it.

Item. A Casula called "a chesipul" of red velvet, with Alb, Amice, Stole and fanons; with parures of red silk.

Item. One other set of frontals for the altar of the blessed Marie in the chapel, of stained cloth with its ridells.

Item. A Chasuble and all that belongs to it of silk for the Chapel of the blessed Marie worked with the blessed Marie lying in childbed.

Item. Another old Chasuble with an Alb and all that belongs to it for weekdays.

Item. A very old cope of cloth of gold.

Item. Two other sets of frontals, one for the altar of Saint Michael, and the other for the altar of the chapel of the blessed Marie of blue, and another of stained cloth with the history of Saint Michael, the work of which is much worn.

Item. A very old frontal for an altar, of blue silk with stars of gold worked on it, and an image of the Crucifixion in the centre.

Item. A small coffer standing upon the altar containing divers relics of Saints, namely, some of the milk of Saint Marie the Virgin.

The jaw bone of Saint Mansuetus.

An arm bone of Saint Felix Martyr.

A certain jaw bone of Saint Appolin Virgin and Martyr.

Some of the stones of the sepulchre of our Lord Jesu Christ.

A portion of the girdle of the blessed Marie the Virgin.

A fragment of a bone of the finger of Saint Agapill the Martyr, with other sacred relics.

Item. Three linen cloths, namely, altar cloths for the principal altar.

Item. Three linen cloths for the altar of the blessed Marie.

Item. Three linen cloths for the altar of the Crucified Jesus.
Two banners of tapestry of Arras, the gift of Fitzhugh.

Item. A cross of bronze parcel gilt to bear before processions; it is very old.

And in the great chamber is a coffer broken in the middle with two keys of iron, not locked; in which are the deeds belonging to the said Priors.

Item. Another old coffer, locked, with a key.

Item. Another coffer, the lid of which is not fastened, in which are candles for pilgrims.

Item. In the great hall a long table with two old Tressels.

All the aforesaid the before written William holds from the day of the writing of these presents until the end of twenty years...according as is fully set forth in certain other indentures between the aforesaid Abbess and Convent and Sir William.

Item that the said William under his own hand has agreed to deliver again all the above specified unto the Abbess and Convent, in as good a state as the said William received them, allowance being made for use during the period. To witness to these things the parties aforesaid of both parts have set their hands and seals to this indenture.

Given the day and year above written.

Endorsed on the back—"Cornubia. An indenture of ornaments and jewels delivered to the Archpriest of Sent Michels Mounte".

From the indenture we can form a fairly accurate conception of the church and its furniture. In the church itself were three altars, the high altar in the middle flanked by those of St Michael and the Crucified Saviour. On the high altar stood a tabernacle and a box containing the relics. The image of St Michael probably stood in his sanctuary near the entrance. Suspended from the roof in front of the high altar was the pyx containing the Host; with a canopy of silk. There were sets of vestments for each of the three altars. The Lady Chapel had its own furniture and frontals. Provision was made that the use of Sarum should be followed in every respect even to the Legenda. Sir Henry Fitzhugh, whose name appears among those to whom the king had committed in 1424 the Mount for conveyance to the abbess, had provided arras and banners for the sanctuary of the Crucifixion. The mention of this gift may perhaps suggest a renovation of the entire *instrumenta*. The relics include the jaw-bone of St Appolin Virgin and Martyr and the arm-bone of St Felix. The story of

St Appolin or Apollonia of Alexandria is said to rest upon a foundation of fact. She was a maiden of great personal charm. Upon her refusal to worship the recognised idol of the city, all her beautiful teeth were pulled out one by one and her body cast to the flames. She is the patroness against toothache. Of St Felix little is known, save that he was one of the patrons of the church in which St Ambrose saw the vision which revealed the identity of two equally obscure saints, St Gervasius and St Protasius. Felix is said to have died for the faith in the reign of Diocletian.

Only one of the above mentioned ornaments requires a word of explanation—*the pax of silver called paxbreyde*. No ceremonial act of the Christian Church can claim the warrant of greater or more widespread antiquity than the kiss of peace which signified the love of the Christian community one for another. At first, men kissed men and women women. Later, it became the custom to pass round some article for each to kiss in turn.[1] This was called the paxbreyde. From the inventory we learn that at St Michael's Mount the paxbreyde was made of silver.

The dissolution of alien priories placed a great amount of patronage, tithe and lands in the king's hands, and, although the intentions of both the king and his ministers were inspired by good will towards the Church, they appear to have displayed ignorance

---

[1] Bp. Frere, *Religious Ceremonial*, p. 117. Two interesting examples of the pax will be found described and illustrated in the *Antiquaries Journal*, x, 356, and xi, 285–6.

and incompetence in the discharge of their duties. St Michael's Mount and its possessions were claimed by the college of St Mary and St Nicholas (now King's College), Cambridge, and it was not until the year 1468 that the college finally relinquished its claim.[1] On the strength, however, of a lease about to be executed by the provost and scholars of the college in 1462,[2] Elizabeth, Abbess of St Saviour and St Mary and St Bridget of Syon, had obtained a grant by letters patent of the priory of St Michael's Mount and its possessions, subject to a condition that prayers were offered for the good estate of the king and Cecily, his mother, and for their souls after death, and those of Richard, late Duke of York, his father, and his progenitors and to do other works of piety.[3] The grant was confirmed by parliament ten years afterwards.[4]

THE ARCHPRESBYTERY

The appointment of William Morton to be the first archpriest of the Mount proved to be a very wise one. It was probably on his initiative that the construction of a breakwater at the Mount was undertaken.

Four months after his visit—on August 10th—the bishop granted an indulgence to assist in the work. In it he recited that at a place called "Mountys Bay" every year many ships and boats were exposed to great danger for lack (*pro defectu*) of a causeway and

1 Close Rolls, 8 Edward IV, m. 29. 2 *Ibid.* 2 Edward IV, m. 28.
3 Pat. Rolls, 1 Edward IV, Nov. 29th, 1461.
4 *Ibid.* 4 Henry VI, Feb. 21st.

seafarers suffered shipwreck and death. The men of Marketjew had begun to construct a causeway of stone, behind which ships could at all times seek refuge, but, owing to their poverty, they could not, without the assistance of the faithful, complete their work. They had appealed to him to grant a letter testimonial on the subject. The bishop therefore, confiding in the infinite pity of Almighty God and of the Blessed Virgin Mary His mother, and in the merits and prayers of the blessed Apostles Peter and Paul, his patrons, and of all the saints, grants forty days' indulgence to those of his diocese (*parochianis*) and others, reckoned as such, who repenting of and confessing their sins, shall give, bequeath or in any way contribute towards the construction of the said causeway.[1]

Whether any substantial benefit accrued from the bishop's indulgence is not known. The task was harder and more costly than had been anticipated. In 1427 William Morton appealed to the king. In his appeal he showed that between the headland (*fronteram*) called the "forlond of Lysard" and the headland called "le forlond of the Londesende of Engelond", there was a great course of sea called Mount's Bay which contained no harbour for ships of eighty tons, whereby many ships were lost, and that he was building a certain road or jetty of stone there, which would make a handy haven for 200 ships of any tonnage, which work had been costly and could not be completed without the king's help.

[1] *Exeter Episcopal Registers, Lacy,* ii, 512.

Wherefore, by advice and consent of the lords spiritual and temporal, the king granted to the said William and to the governors of the work for the time being, quayage for seven years as follows: viz. from every vessel of 120 tons and over, anchoring by the Mount, 12*d.*, between 120 and 60 tons, 8*d.*; and under 60 tons, 4*d.*, so often as they anchored; and from every strange fishing boat fishing in the said bay for the fish called "hake" in the season of fishing for the same 12*d.* yearly or hake of that value; to be applied under the survey of four of the most sufficient men chosen from among the merchants of Marghasieu and fishermen belonging to the said jetty, by the other merchants and fishermen.[1]

William Morton's impress is also found upon the dues payable by the conventionary tenants of the Meneage. Half a century later, in a compotus roll, Vivian Treonney, deputy receiver of the Mount, refers to a commutation, amounting to 35*s.* 10*d.* of dues payable to the Mount by the conventionary tenants in Meneage, effected by Mr William Morton, chaplain and archpriest. The dues were apparently for the purpose of works or repairs. Of that sum it is stated that 21*s.* 10*d.* has been rendered in the form of 131 capons and the rest (14*s.*) has been expended in accordance with Morton's directions. In 1482, when the roll was made, a capon appears to have been worth 2*d.* It is not stated what became of the capons. At that time the salaried officials were Mr Ralph Crabbe, archpriest, whose stipend was 10 marks, i.e.

[1] Pat. Rolls, 6 Henry VI, and *Ancient Petitions*, No. 6187.

£1. 13s. 4d., two chaplains—William Michell and Richard Hooper, who were paid nine marks each; a clerk, Richard Duke by name, who received seven marks; a receiver, whose salary was ten marks, and a supervisor—Mr John Harpecote, who received seven marks.

A compotus roll of 1432 of William Morton shows that, probably owing to the heavy expenses incurred in the construction of the breakwater, there was owing to the Exchequer by Robert Hay £19. 13s. 10d., by William Morton £44. 11s. 6d., and by John Godolphin, £63. 6s. 8d.

.   .   .   .   .   .

During his visit to Cornwall in 1478, William of Worcester made it his business to consult the kalendars of churches and religious houses for obits of benefactors and lists of such saints as were had in special remembrance. At St Michael's Mount he does not appear to have found any of the former, and his list of the latter, exclusive of St Bryehan and his twenty-four so-called sons and daughters, all of whose names are given, though without dates of their commemoration, consists of the following:

St Wilfrid, Bishop; on the morrow of St George.
St Petrock, Confessor; on June 4th.
St Hilda, Virgin; on August 23rd.
St Hermes, Confessor; on August 28th.
Translation of St Birinus, Bishop; on the day of St Cuthbert.

[1]St...Majore, Martyr, on November 11th.

St Nonnita, Mother of St David, who lies at the Church of Altarnon, six miles from Launceston, where St David was born.

Three of these, Wilfrid, Hilda and Birinus are Saxon. Petrock, Hermes and Nonnita are Cornish.

St Petrock is rightly regarded as the founder of the famous monastery of Bodmin even if we suppose—as seems probable—that Padstow was the spot chosen for it by the saint. A life of St Petrock, written in the eleventh or twelfth century, has been recently translated and published by Canon G. H. Doble.

Of Hermes little is known. Three saints at least are said to have borne that name, one of whom was chosen as patron of a chapel in St Hilary parish, in 1309 licensed for Divine Service by Bishop Stapledon.

William of Worcester's note respecting the birthplace of St David is very remarkable. It is perhaps fortunate for him that he is now beyond the reach of those who, relying upon the testimony of Rhygyvarch, their fellow-countryman, regard Cardiganshire as the place of his nativity. Rhygyvarch's *Life of St David* has been translated and edited by the Rev. A. W. Wade Evans.[2]

The remaining three whom William found in the kalendar are all historical personages. Birinus was consecrated by the Archbishop of Milan and became

[1] November 11th is the Feast of St Martin of Tours, but he was not a martyr. The entry is obscure.

[2] S.P.C.K. 1923.

Bishop of Dorchester-on-Thames. In the year 634 he was sent to convert the West Saxons. As the result of his mission Cynegils, their king, believed and was baptised.

St Wilfrid, Saxon by birth, was brought up at the Celtic monastery of Lindisfarne. As the result of a visit to Rome he became attached to Roman customs and was their protagonist at the famous conference held at the abbey of Whitby under the presidency of the Abbess Hilda in the year 664. The matter in dispute was whether Roman or Celtic customs should prevail. Colman, Bishop of Lindisfarne, and the Abbess Hilda favoured the latter; Agilbert, Bishop of the West Saxons, and Wilfrid, the former. The chief points of difference were the date of Easter and the tonsure of the priest.[1] The result of the conference was inconclusive. The Celts did not yield until forty years afterwards. Colman, dissatisfied with the decision retired to Iona and Wilfrid was elected in his place, but during his prolonged absence in Gaul whither he had gone to receive consecration, Chad was appointed, but he afterwards gave way in favour of Wilfrid. The Archbishop, Theodore, intervened and decided to split up the Lindisfarne bishopric into four separate dioceses. Wilfrid resisted, was imprisoned and banished. It was not until 681 that he began his great work among the South Saxons.

The Abbess Hilda who had presided at the conference and whose expectations had been disappointed by the decision arrived at—such as it was—

[1] *The Celtic Christianity of Cornwall*, pp. 50–8.

nevertheless continued to fulfil her vocation at Whitby, in the words of the venerable Bede,

teaching the strict observance of justice, piety and chastity and other virtues, and especially peace and charity...and in the year of our Lord 680 on the 17th of November this most religious servant of Christ, the Abbess Hilda, having suffered under an infirmity for seven years, and having performed many heavenly works on earth, died, and was carried into Paradise by the angels.

It is not difficult to account for the choice of the three last-named saints for commemoration at the altar of St Michael's Mount. After the suppression of the monastery by King Henry V, the Abbess of Syon, though not directly responsible for the conduct of Divine Service there, was lady paramount, and doubtless took an interest in all that went on. She was presumably English and conversant with the history of the critical days of the seventh century when the Roman and Celtic ideals were brought into competition. Her choice, if it was her choice, as is most probable, was singularly wise and well timed, suggesting, as it did, the peaceful solution of a problem which had confronted churchmen and statesmen alike from generation to generation, namely, how to bring the two races into whole-hearted cooperation in matters ecclesiastical and civil.

From 1478, with the exception of the Roll of 1482, we have no official information respecting the religious life of the Mount until the reign of Henry VIII. From what is hereafter said of pilgrimages it

will be inferred that the chaplain made great efforts
to encourage them, and whatever offerings were
made before the image of St Michael were not at the
disposal of the chaplains who, as we have seen, were
each paid a definite sum by way of stipend, but
served to swell the balance paid to the Abbess of Syon.

It is well known to our readers that not the least
important of those statutes by which the papal
authority was abolished in England was that of
1533–4 which, *inter alia*, forbade the application to
Rome for faculties, dispensations and the like and
vested the dispensing power in the Archbishop of
Canterbury—a statute which was confirmed by Act
of Parliament three years later. In the case of dispensations of a novel kind it was provided that they
were not to be granted without licence from the king
or the council.

In 1537 John Arscott, Archpriest of St Michael's
Mount, was granted by Archbishop Cranmer a dispensation enabling him to hold, in addition to his
office as archpriest, another cure or benefice, such as
was usually assigned to a secular clerk, provided that
as archpriest he had not the cure of souls and as such
his income did not amount to eight pounds when all
accustomed deductions had been made. The dispensation was subject to ratification by the king and the
issue of the king's letters patent confirming the same.
In 1537 Arscott was presented by the Abbess of
Syon to the living of St Clement near Truro.

It would be foolish and untrue to say that the
monastic system, as it existed in the sixteenth century,

did not call for reform or that the revenues of the religious houses were not in some cases excessive and misapplied; but the manner in which they were suppressed and the uses to which their revenues were devoted afford one of the darkest pages of English Church history. Wolsey, whom no one can accuse of disloyalty to the Church, with the foresight of a statesman and reformer, contemplated the erection and endowment of colleges for the study of theology, law and medicine and, by the suppression of some of the smaller and less useful monasteries for the purpose, had become the founder of Christ Church and the College of Physicians. This diversion of monastic endowments to purposes, equally if not more beneficent, was made a precedent for the suppression of all monasteries, whether great or small, well or ill governed, in order to administer to the unbounded and licentious extravagance of the king and his court.

This was effected by means most foul and cruel. The religious houses were visited by commissioners of doubtful character, and inventories were made of their ornaments and furniture. In many cases their valuables were already ear-marked before the returns were sent in. It is often difficult to determine when, how and by whom the inventories were made. That of St Michael's Mount is undated and unsigned, and we are therefore unable to state whether the archpresbytery was suppressed as a priory or as an appanage of Syon Abbey. It is probable that the inventory was made in the autumn of the year 1535 and the valuables sent to London, and the plunder of the church legalised by the Act of Dissolution passed in the following February. The inventory is here given in full, the spelling and arrangement being slightly altered for convenience of reference.

	Weight
JEWELS	
First. A Pyx wherein the Blessed Sacrament is reserved.	3¼ oz.
Item. A Canopy over the Sacrament of silver and parcel gilt with a Crown of silver	13¼ oz.
Item. A Monstrance of silver gilt with a beryl in the middle for the Sacrament in procession.	9¼ oz.
Item. Another Monstrance of silver gilt that came from my Lady Abbess.	34 oz.
Item. An Image of St Michael of silver gilt	10 oz.
Item. Two Bonnets for St Michael, the one of tinsel satin the fore part embroidered with gold and a pearl, the other of blue velvet fringed with gold and (inlaid) with goldsmith's work of silver and gold.	3¼ oz.
Item. Two Coats for St Michael, the one of cloth of gold and the other of purple velvet embroidered with I.H.S.	
Item. A Chain of gold.	4¼ oz.
Item. A Flower like a rose, of gold of Venice set with pearl and stone, and a little Bell of silver and gilt.	¾ oz.
Item. A Baldrick of silver and gilt for St Michael.	3 oz.
Item. A Cross of silver and gilt with Mary and John.	62 oz.

Item. A foot for the same of copper and gilt.

Item. A part of the Holy Cross enclosed in silver,
   double gilt. $12\frac{1}{4}$ oz.

Item. Another part of the Holy Cross enclosed in
   silver, double gilt, with a beryl. $2\frac{1}{4}$ oz. and 20 dwt.

Item. A Pax of silver and gilt. $10\frac{1}{4}$ oz.

Item. A Pair of Cruets of silver. $7\frac{3}{4}$ oz.

Item. Seven chalices whereof 4 are gilt and 3
   parcel gilt.   115   oz.

Item. One Censer of silver.   13   oz.

Item. A Ship of silver for frankincense and a little
   spoon of silver. $8\frac{1}{4}$ oz.

Item. A Box of timber gilt, with divers relics of Martyrs and
   Saints.

Item. A Cloth of purple velvet with an image of St Bridget
   embroidered, and 49s. 2d. of money upon it and a ship of
   silver.

Item. Four gold Rings, three of them with stones, and the
   fourth....

Item. Two cloths hanging beside St Michael with an Image
   of St Michael and 43s. 6d. in money upon it and Five
   Ships of silver, 43 rings of silver, a Plate of silver with a
   Woman's Image upon it and an Image of silver kneeling,
   and divers other small Images and tokens of silver upon it.

Item. Upon the same a royal, 4 nobles and 2 ducats of gold,
   a ring of gold valued at 10s., a little image of St Michael of
   gold valued at 51s. 8d.

Item. A little Cloth with the Crucifixion and 4s. 9d. of
   money, six rings of silver and a...of silver.

Item. A pair of Beads of amber banded with jasper valued at
20*d*.

Item. A Monstrance of silver gilt with relics that
came from My Lady.   24 oz

Item. A Sword and a pair of spurs of copper and
gilt that was King Henry of Windsor's.

Item. Two pairs of latten Candlesticks for an
Altar.

Item. Two branched Candlesticks with the lights.

Item. The jaw-bone of Saint Appolyen enshrined
in silver and gilt.   10 oz.

Item. A Bible, written, with a clasp of silver; a
Primer of parchment, written, with a clasp of
silver; also...written in parchment.

ORNAMENTS IN THE CHURCH

First. Seven Corporal cases with the corporals whereof three
of cloth of gold, one of black velvet, one of red velvet, one of
black satin and another of red satin, all embroidered.

Item. Four pairs of Curtains whereof two pairs are of silk
and two pairs of linen cloth.

Item. Four Frontals for the high altar, whereof one of red
velvet embroidered with clouds and sickles, one of white
satin fringed with white damask, one of red sarcenet embroidered with clouds and *Jes. Chr.* and another of blue
cloth of bawdkyn and one cloth for the border of the same.

Item. Six copes, whereof one of green cloth of gold with a
clasp silver and gilt; one of blue damask embroidered with
flowers of gold; another of blue cloth of bawdkyn with
orphreys embroidered; two of white cloth of bawdkyn

lined with candasron; one of white linen cloth with orphreys of shot sarcenet for Lent, and two tunicks for Lent of the same suit.

Item. A Frontal for Lent for the high altar of white cloth with a cross of shot sarcenet.

Item. Two pewter Basins with four Cruets and a latten Censer.

Item. Ten pairs of Vestments whereof one of blue velvet embroidered with flowers and two Tunicks to the same; another of murray velvet; one of white satin; one of red cloth of bawdkyn; one of red damask; one of green satin; one of blue damask; one of green cloth of bawdkyn for every day; and one pair of white damask the orphreys of red sarcenet.

Item. Four Frontals for the by altars whereof three of sarcenet with clouds and the other painted.

Item. Two chests for the Copes and Vestments.

Item. Four Mass-books whereof two be printed and the others be written.

Item. In our Lady chapel three frontals two of white bawdkyn, the one panelled with tawny velvet, the other panelled with blue bawdkyn and one painted.

Item. Three pairs of Vestments whereof one of white damask the orphreys of red damask; one of green chamlett and another of bawdkyn.

Item. A Mass-book written in parchment; two pairs of "Orgayns"; two coffers, the one for vestments, the other with certain books of the monk's use; a processional Cross of copper and a banner painted for the same; a Cross staff of timber gilded and a Banner for the same.

Item. Books in the quire, a Legenda, an antiphonal, a breviary written and noted on parchment; two service books of parchment, one of stories, the other of feasts; a Legend in print; a manual in print; a glossed psalter of parchment written and noted; two legends written on parchment; two psalters written on parchment; six processioners whereof four are written on parchment and two in print; two hymnals written on parchment; sixteen books of... and a legendary.

Item. Twelve albs of linen cloth; sixteen altar cloths, twelve plain and 4 diaper; six wiping towels; two cloths of red velvet with sules (? streaks) of gold for the sepulchre; four chaplets two of cloth of gold and the other two of blue velvet and with another of silver and all embroidered with pearl.

HABILIMENTS OF WAR

First. Four bows of yew and thirteen sheaves of arrows, four sallets, two breastplates, a pair of splints, two pairs of breastplates of copper; three "pott germys" of brass with eight "chamberons"; two slings with four chamberons; two "seroyntyns" and two hagebusthis; three hand guns and a firkin of gunpowder; four bills and three old poleaxes of iron.

Item. A pair of coral beads (rosary) gawded with three set of silver with two rings and a pair of slippers of silver weighing $3\frac{1}{2}$ ounces.

Item. A pair of coral beads gawded with three set of silver, $1\frac{1}{2}$ ounces.

Item. Three corporals with the cases, two green, one with I.H.S. and the other with C.H.R. embroidered with gold, the three of blue damask embroidered with a crowned I.H.S.

Item. Five Vestments with all their apparel, one of them of blue worsted, the orphreys of red bawdekin, one of old cloth of gold of loom work, the orphreys of cloth of gold, one of murray velvet embroidered with "pawnnes" the orphreys of cloth of tissue; one of old cloth of bawdkyn of blue and red, the orphreys of green and red, one of white branched (brocade) silk, the orphreys of cloth of bawdkyn.

Item. Divers pieces for the sepulchre whereof one painted of the resurrection and orphreys embroidered with imagery; one other frontal of crimson velvet with flowers of gold; two altar cloths of red sarcenet, one with a frontlet all embroidered with clouds.

Item. A frontal of white satin and green velvet empannelled with fringe of the same and three roses embroidered.

Item. A Cope of purple velvet embroidered with pansies, the orphreys of blue gold of tissue.

Item. A "pere" of crimson velvet with orphreys of silk for the sepulchre.

Item. Four silk towels to bear the patens at Mass time, two of green, one of cream colour and the other of wrought work.

Item. Two palls for hearses, one of bawdkyn with lions of gold the other of blue serge with crosses of linen cloth for the same.

Item. A coverlet to hang behind the sepulchre of greenish colour.

Item. A veil for Lent of red canvas painted.

Item. Five painted cloths to hang before Saints in Lent.

Item. A "soan" cloth of blue silk with the Trinity on the one side and our Lady, Saints Bridget and Katharine of Swath on the other side.

Item. Two white silk cloths for the Font, the one damask, the other bawdkyn.

Item. Six altar cloths, two diaper and four plain cloth.

Item. Seven coarse cloths to cover the altars.

Item. Eight wiping towels.

Item. A pair of beads of silver with seven beads of red coral, all weighing five ounces.

Item. A pair of coral beads gawded with three set of silver and divers stones in the hanging, enclosed in silver, all weighing $5\frac{1}{4}$ ounces.

Item. A green corse (corpse cloth) barred with silver, all weighing $6\frac{1}{4}$ ounces.

Comparing the inventories of 1337, 1430 and 1535 it will be noticed that the furniture and ornaments have increased in value and variety. So long as the priory was affiliated to Mont St Michel there was little to distinguish the church from that of an ordinary parish. The image of St Michael naturally occupied an honoured place. A hundred years later there were costly vestments, frontals and four altars— the high altar and those of St Michael and of the Crucifixion in the church itself, besides that of Our Lady in her chapel. We find also relics, some of them objectionable and the others of small importance. During the century which followed an immense accretion of ornaments has been gathered. The more objectionable relics have been laid aside, but two

portions of the holy Cross have found their way
thither. St Michael, as is meet, occupies his accustomed place and the jaw-bone of St Apollonia still
receives the homage of those who suffer from toothache. A most interesting addition has been made to
the treasury, to wit, the sword and spurs of the ill-
fated Henry VI. These, at any rate, were genuine and
no one will begrudge the homage paid to one who
went through so great tribulation. If historians have
found little to admire in the person and character of
Henry of Windsor, Cambridge and Eton have to
thank him for the foundation of two of our most
famous seats of learning. It will be remembered that
St Michael's Mount and its possessions narrowly
escaped annexation to the former.[1] Henry was quite
unfitted for the responsibilities of high office, but no
one has ever seriously questioned the depth and
sincerity of his religious convictions, the purity of his
life or the reality and extent of his benevolence. At a
time of national disappointment and chagrin, secret
intrigue and internal strife, he was politically only so
much flotsam tossed to and fro on a stormy sea.
Nevertheless, there was that about him which secured
for him in his lifetime a devotion to his person, and
after his death a reverence for his piety such as no
English king had won save Edward the Confessor.
He was regarded as a saint and in after years his name
was invoked by those in dire distress. A list of
miracles wrought in his name was collected and sub-

[1] King's College which originally bore the name of St Mary and
St Nicholas. See p. 71.

mitted for investigation with a view to his canonisation. Of these miracles two only are connected with Cornwall. The first concerns Richard Whitby, described as a priest of St Michael's Mount, who, as the result of a pilgrimage made to the tomb of Blessed King Henry, claimed to have been miraculously healed of a fever of long duration, which had reduced him to a skeleton. After examination this claim was disallowed. The second case, that of Richard Vyvian, described as of Penzance "in the parish of St Paternus" was similar to the former. Vyvian, smitten by a plague and thought by all to be at death's door, was most miraculously delivered by the prayers of Blessed King Henry (*beati regis Henrici...liberatus*). No investigation appears to have been made in this case.[1] It appears to have been customary in the fifteenth century for pilgrims to place their offerings in a box which stood near the statue of St Michael.

The last inventory gives the amount of jewellery and money found on the cloths hanging beside the images of St Michael and St Bridget. The beads mentioned were probably rosaries, strings of beads "gawded", that is, furnished with ornamented or larger stones to mark the incidence of the Lord's Prayer in the Act of Devotion. Easter sepulchres were not uncommon in Cornwall and some are still to be found, for example, at St Just in Penwith, Wendron and St Germans. They were niches in the north wall of the sanctuary, in which a portion of the Blessed

[1] The MSS. in the British Museum has been translated and edited by Father Ronald Knox and Shane Leslie.

Sacrament was reserved from Good Friday evening until Easter morning. The "dressing up" of St Michael with bonnet, coat and baldrick was a bit of fancy ritual, harmless enough in itself, but perhaps better adapted for a fair or holiday than for the purpose of religion. Shakespeare may have had some such thought in his mind when he wrote:

> The summer's flower is to the summer sweet,
> Though to itself it only live and die,
> But if that flower with base infection meet,
> The basest weed outbraves his dignity.
> > For sweetest things turn sourest by their deeds.
> > Lilies that fester smell far worse than weeds.

The castle, church, lands, advowsons, tithes, dues and emoluments of whatsoever kind were confiscated and taken into the king's hands to be disposed of as he thought fit. In some cases long leases had been granted, and until their expiration the lands were withheld from sale. The advowson of St Hilary was granted by Queen Elizabeth in the year 1565 to William Milliton of Pengersick; that of St Clement near Truro has remained in the crown until now. The manors of Lambesso and Traboe, the church, castle and Mount with the fairs at Marketjew were together granted in 1599 to Thomas Bellott and John Budden acting as agents for Robert, Earl of Salisbury, for the sum of £3114. 9s. 6d. By William his son, the second Earl, the manor of Traboe was in 1651 sold to John Gregor, and the manor of Lambesso in 1666 to Sir James Smyth.

In 1640 William, Earl of Salisbury, sold the manors of St Michael's Mount and the manor of Marketjew with the fairs and markets and tithes in Penzance, Alverton, Pencobone, Enhellow, Tehidy, Reskageage, Madron, Camborne, Gwithian and Illogan and all tithes of fish in Mount's Bay, Marketjew, St Hilary, Newlyn and Mousehole to Francis Basset of Tehidy, Esq.[1]

By recovery and fine[2] the Bassets conveyed the same in 1659 to John St Aubyn, Esq., in whose family the Mount and the aforesaid possessions have remained until the present time. While other and greater monasteries, like Tavistock and Tywardreath, have been left without one stone upon another, that of St Michael's Mount, owing in some measure to its commanding position, but chiefly to the loving care of its owners, still affords abundant evidence of its past as a priory, a fortress and a home.

[1] Pat. Rolls, 1640.
[2] Fines Hil., 1656, and Easter 1659.

Humphry Arundell

THE dissolution of the lesser monasteries throughout the kingdom began in the year 1536 under an Act of Parliament passed at the instance of the king.[1] In the same year Convocation enacted a canon promulgated by the crown which transferred the dedication festivals of churches to the first Sunday in October, forbade the compulsory cessation from labour on patronal festivals and the observance of any festivals in harvest time except the feasts of apostles, the Blessed Virgin Mary and St George. The object of this injunction was to enable the farmer to gather in his harvest. It was, however, popularly misinterpreted to mean the abrogation of the holy days and provoked great indignation throughout the country.

At St Keverne a fisherman, Carnepyssack by name, instructed a painter to prepare a banner in which they would have the picture of Christ with His wounds abroad and a banner in His hand, Our Lady on the one side holding her breast in her hand, St John the Baptist on the other side, the king's grace and the queen kneeling, and all the commonalty kneeling with scripture above their heads, making their petition to the picture of Christ that it would please the king's grace that they might have their holidays. Carnepyssack was reported to have said that he and

[1] 27 Henry VIII, cap. 28.

his fellows had bought two hundred jerkins and that they would carry the banner on Pardon Monday.

Sir William Godolphin, who was in constant correspondence with Cromwell, vicar-general or vice-gerent, recommended that the regulation concerning holidays should be relaxed, and that Carnepyssack should be hanged in chains at Helston. Owing to the plague, no assize could be held at Launceston and the trial of the culprit was postponed. In the same letter in which this news is conveyed to Cromwell Sir William informs him that a fight has taken place in Mount's Bay between Sir John Dudley and Sir George Carew and four Frenchmen which lasted from 5 p.m. until dark. Sir William heard the shooting. But for a great tempest which rose at night and the breaking of Sir John Dudley's sprit-mast they had taken all four. "At daybreak they brought one into the key of the Mount all to broken and departed to sea in good health and angry to God to send them such weather."[1] It is not clear whether the Act of Parliament for dissolving the lesser monasteries suppressed the priory of St Michael's Mount which, since the days of Henry V, had consisted of an arch-priest and two chaplains.

Three years later (1539) when the abbey of Syon was dissolved and its possessions confiscated, the revenues of the Mount and its government were granted by King Henry VIII to Humphry Arundell, who must not be identified with his uncle and namesake, who was one of the collectors of the subsidy in 1524.

[1] State Papers, 29 Henry VIII, Aug. 28th.

Humphry Arundell, Governor of the Mount, was the son of Roger Arundell of Helland and a nephew of Sir John Arundell of Lanherne. He was born in the year 1513,[1] and succeeded to a considerable estate on the death of his mother in 1537. The suppression of the greater monasteries was followed ten years later by the imposition of the English Prayer Book, and the spoliation and destruction of church ornaments produced widespread alarm. The embers of revolt in the Meneage district still smouldered and only awaited the breeze of opportunity to burst into flame.

This came in 1548 when William Body,[2] the proctor of Thomas Wynter, Archdeacon of Cornwall, and a supposed illegitimate son of Cardinal Wolsey, set about the reformation of religion in the county which took the form of destroying images and other ornaments and the suppression of practices to which the people were deeply attached. Over a thousand persons assembled at Helston. Body was attacked thereupon and murdered in his lodging, and a proclamation issued in which the rebels demanded the laws of Henry VIII and none other until the king attained the age of twenty-three years, and declared that those

[1] Inq. p.m. Joan Arundell, 29 Henry VIII.
[2] A lease dated April 14th, 1544, was granted by the bishop, John Pollard, Archdeacon of Cornwall and the Dean and Chapter of Exeter to William Body, described as late of London, one of the Gentlemen Ushers of the King's Privy Chamber, of all the Archdeaconry of Cornwall, the prebend in Glasney College annexed to it and the advowson of the Hospital of St John in Helston for 34 years at £10 rent. C. Henderson, *Journ. Roy. Inst. of Cornwall*, XXII, 405.

who would defend Body, or follow such new fashions as he did, should be punished in like manner. The ringleaders of this faction were Martin Geoffrey, priest of St Keverne, John Kylter, yeoman, William Kylter, husbandman, John Piers, mariner, and Edmund Irish, smith. Two days later the rebels numbering 5000 threatened to be present at the sessions about to be held at Helston, which were in consequence postponed. This rising nevertheless was soon quelled by the local authorities. Geoffrey and twelve others were found guilty of treason and executed.[1] Comedy succeeds tragedy. Body's widow married one John Tyssard, who thereupon claimed to be archdeacon. The Bishop of Exeter appealed to the Privy Council, who commanded the Dean of Exeter to summon the cathedral chapter in order to discover how the archdeaconry came to be leased to Body and who sealed the lease. Tyssard was summoned before the council and, after examination, was commanded not to intermeddle with any part of the archdeaconry "bycause he hath very ungodly and unlawfully used the office of the same".[2]

It will be remembered that the Act of Uniformity authorising the use of the first English Prayer Book and forbidding any other use was ordered to come into force on Whitsunday, June 9th, 1549. The following day the people of Sampford Courtenay rose in insurrection against the new order. It was essentially a popular rising which rapidly spread from parish to

---

[1] *Baga de Secretis*, pouch 15, m. 14.
[2] *Acts of the P.C.* III, 419, 454, 494.

parish. Its officers at first were a tailor, a shoemaker, a labourer and a fish-driver. Very soon, however, it could reckon among its leaders representatives of the oldest and wealthiest families in the West. The rebellion was in full swing in Devon before the Cornish came in. Humphry Arundell, Governor of the Mount, John Wideslade of Tregarrick and his son William, Nicholas Boyer, Mayor of Bodmin, and Thomas Holmes, yeoman of Blisland, were among the most prominent of its leaders in this county. The gentlemen of Cornwall who held aloof with their wives sought refuge from the rebels at Trematon Castle and at St Michael's Mount. It is presumed that Arundell was at Helland when the insurrection broke out. St Michael's Mount was besieged by the rebels. The besiegers crossed over at low water bearing great trusses of hay wherewith to "blench the defendants' sight and dead their shot", and were not long in forcing an entrance. All who were captured were sent to Bodmin, the headquarters of the rebels. Trematon was captured and Sir Richard Grenville seized while holding a parley with them. Cornwall was soon altogether in their hands. Exeter and its neighbourhood became the battle-ground. Lord Russell, Sir Gawen and Sir Peter Carew were the chief commanders of the king's forces. After a most determined and bloody struggle in which the Cornish under Arundell performed feats of valour which won the admiration of their enemies, the rebels were finally defeated at Clist Heath on July 21st, 1549.

Humphry Arundell escaped to Launceston, where he hoped to wreak vengeance upon Sir Richard Grenville and others who were imprisoned there. Their gaolers, however, instead of handing over Grenville captured Arundell. It was left to Lord Russell's discretion to deal with the rebel prisoners. He sent up to the council Sir Thomas Pomeroy, Humphry Arundell, John and William Winslade and six others. Of these Arundell, John Winslade, Thomas Holmes and John Bury of Silverton were transferred to the Tower. They were tried on November 26th, 1549, and, having pleaded guilty of levying war against the king, were hanged at Tyburn in the following January. An inquisition held after Arundell's death showed that he held the manors of Cassacawn, Helleset and Penryn Borough, the advowson of Helland and the manor of Trevethow Lelant, leased to Ralph Michell, all of which were forfeited by his attainder. There is no mention of St Michael's Mount, from which it is inferred that his interest in it was purely official.

An element of romance hangs around and about the family of Winslade of Tregarrick and Bochym, both of which estates fell to the crown as the result of John Winslade's participation in the rebellion. Like the family of Copplestone of Lametton, its head was an esquire of the White Spur. Concerning this order Spelman says that these esquires were created by the king, being invested with a silver collar of S.S. and a pair of silver spurs, whence they were called White Spurs. By reason of the attainder of John Winslade the family was reduced to the direst poverty.[1] Of William Winslade, son of the said John, Richard Carew the historian, who was born only six years after Winslade's execution, relates: "Winslade's sonne led a walking life, with his harpe, to gentlemen's houses where through, and by his other active qualities he was entitled Sir Tristram; neither wanted he, as some say, a belle Isound (Iseult) the more aptly to resemble his patterne". The mention of Tristan and Iseult in this connection is very interesting. If the two lovers, in the romance, formed the burden of his song, one can only regret that he left no issue to preserve the tradition.

To Richard Carew we also owe the gruesome stories of the Mayor of Bodmin and of the miller who were implicated in the rebellion.[2]

And among other the offenders in this rebellion I thought it well to note twaine for the manner of their execution seemed straunge. The First was one Bowyer, who was Maior of a towne in Cornewall called Bodmyn. This Maior had bene

[1] An exemplification of letters patent granted in September 1552 to Reginald Mohun, Esq., of the body of the king recites that John Winslade formerly of Tregarrick, gentleman, who was attainted of high treason was seised before his attainder of the manors of Bochym, Tregarrick, Tolcarne, Penknight (Penkneth), Killiowe, etc., and in 1544 settled these manors upon John Winslade and Agnes, his wife, with remainder to John and his heirs. By his attainder they fell to the crown. Other lands in Kilkhampton, etc., he had, in 1534, granted to Robert Winslade and his issue with reversion to the said John. This reversion also fell to the crown. The letters patent grant to the said John Mohun all the aforementioned lands.

[2] Similar accounts are also to be found in Grafton's *Chronicle*.

busie among the rebelles, but some that loved hym sayd that
he was forced thereunto, and that if he had not contented
them, they would have destroyed him and his house. But
howsoever it was, this was his ende. On a certaine day Sir
Anthony Kingston beyng Provost Marshall in the field wrote
his letter unto the sayde Maior declaring that he and certayne
others with him would come and dine with him such a day.
The Maior seemed to be very joyous thereof, and made for
him very good preparation. And at the time appointed, Sir
Anthony Kingstone with his company came and were right
hartely welcomed to the Maior. And before they sate downe
to dinner, Sir Anthony calling the Maior a syde shewed him
that their must be execution done in that towne, and therefore
willed him with speed to cause a payre of Gallowes to be made,
that the same might be redy by the ende of dinner. The maior
went diligently about it, and caused the same to be done.
When dinner was ended Sir Anthony called the Maior unto
him and asked if that were redy that he spake to him, and he
answered it was redy. Then he tooke the Maior by the hand
and prayed him to bring him to the place where the same was
and so he did. And when Sir Anthony saw them, he sayde
unto the Maior, thinke you they be strong enough? Yea Sir,
sayde he, that they are. Well then sayde Sir Anthony get you
even up to them for they are provided for you; the Maior
cryed I trust you meane no such thing to me. Sir sayth he
there is no remedy, you have bene a busie Rebell and therefore
this is appoynted for your rewarde, so that without longer
respite or tarrying there was the Maior hanged.

And at the same time also and nere unto this place, there
was a Miller who had bene a very busy varlet in that rebellion
whome also Sir Anthony Kingston sought for. But the
Miller had warning, and he having a good tall felow to his

servant called him unto him and sayd, I must go forth, if their come any to ask for me, say that thou art the owner of the Myll, and that thou has kept the same this foure yeres, and in no wise name not me. The servant promised his Maister so to do. Afterwards came Syr Anthony Kingston to the Myllers house and called for the Miller, the servant answered that he was the Miller. Then sayd Maister Kinston how long hast thou kept this Mill and he answered three years. Well then sayde he come on thou must go with me, and caused his servantes to lay handes on him, and brought him to the next tree saiying you have bene a rebellious Knave, and therefore here shall you hang. Then cried he and sayd that he was not the Miller, but the Miller's servaunt, well then sayd he you are a false knave to be in two tales, therefore hange him up sayd he, and so he was hanged. After he was hanged, one beying by sayd to Syr Anthony Kingstone, surely this was but the Miller's man, what then sayd he could he ever have done his Maister better service than to hang for him?

Here we are not concerned with the moral or religious aspect of the rebellion and its consequences. The provocation which led up to it and the punishments which followed are paralleled in other departments of the social and political life of the age. One can only regret that the rebellion was occasioned by an attempt to coerce the consciences of believers, and that in this matter similar attempts have been made from time to time. Experience which, in the ordinary affairs of life, is so useful seems to have failed here to teach a needed lesson.

Pilgrimage

PILGRIMAGE, as an act of piety, has its roots so firmly embedded in the soul of man that we are not surprised to find it occupying a prominent place in mediaeval Christianity. The Israelites were required to be present at the temple services three times in the year, and what are styled the Songs of Degrees[1] appear to have derived their name from the fact that they were sung at various stations by the pilgrims on their way to the holy city. The early Christians gathered around the places sanctified by the blood of the martyrs. The followers of Mahomet go on pilgrimage to Mecca.

No doubt the scenes of the Lord's life and death and the tombs of St Peter and St Paul were the places of the earliest Christian pilgrimage. The finding of the Holy Cross by Helena, mother of Constantine the Great, in the fourth century gave an impetus and a sanction to what was already a common practice.

Pilgrimages were made sometimes to discharge a vow and sometimes to gain an answer to prayer. Englishmen frequented St James of Compostella, St Edward of Westminster, St Thomas of Canterbury and St Joseph of Glastonbury. In Cornwall, St Michael's Mount and St Day were the places of most frequent pilgrimage. Pilgrims were free of toll and their persons inviolable. Each shrine had its own token, a shell or small bell, a trinket of some sort with

[1] Psalms cxx–cxxiv.

a special device, which the pilgrim took home and kept. The forty-three rings mentioned in the inventory of 1535 may have been made for this purpose. The towns of pilgrimage were full of inns and churches. Quite apart from any spiritual advantage which might accrue to the pilgrim, it goes without saying that pilgrimages fostered social intercourse, drew people of every rank and class together and afforded change of life and scene.

The appearance of the archangel, St Michael, to Aubert, Bishop of Avranches, in the year 706 and the command given to him to build a church in *Monte Tumba*—the Norman Mount—led to the erection of the magnificent abbey of Mont St Michel which, begun by Richard, Duke of Normandy, in 966, was completed by William the Conqueror. It is impossible to say when the Celtic monastery or hermitage of the Cornish Mount gave place to a similar establishment. No doubt the one suggested the other, for both were Benedictine houses.

It is equally difficult to say when pilgrimages to the Mount had their beginning. The Celt regarded religion as a high adventure. The Quest of the Graal, the Lives of the Saints and the amazing stories related of their perils, fortitude and heroism, when subjected to severest criticism, remain as evidence of the blind endeavour which ever presses forward towards "the light which never was on sea or land".

The charter of Robert, Count of Mortain, as given in the *Monasticon* and *Cartulary*, is supplemented by (1) a statement to which the seal of Leofric, Bishop of

Exeter, is affixed, that the said charter "was confirmed and ratified (*roborata*) at Pevensel in the month of October in the year 1085, the fourteenth year of indiction",[1] and (2) a grant made by Bishop Leofric, by command of Pope Gregory, of freedom of the church of St Michael from episcopal control and an indulgence for those who visit the church.

The two documents are full of error. For example, Bishop Leofric died in 1073 and Hildebrand did not become pope until that same year. The year 1085 was the eighth year of indiction, and 1073 the eleventh year of indiction. In spite of these obvious blunders it is probable some such charter was granted to Mont St Michel and that, when the priory was finally severed from the abbey, the chaplains who succeeded the monks claimed as their heritage the traditions which had been common to both abbey and priory. In order to give colour to their claim they may have assigned dates to suit their convenience. As the charter implicitly sanctions pilgrimage a translation of it is inserted here.

I Leofric, by the gift of God bishop of Exeter, having been urged to free and exempt so far from all episcopal law, authority or submission, the church of Blessed Michael, the Archangel, of Cornwall, seeing that it is believed and acknowledged to be consecrated and sanctified by the office and ministry of angels, by command and exhortation of my lord

---

[1] The year of indiction is obtained by adding three to the year of Our Lord and dividing the sum by fifteen. The remainder after division is the year of indiction, thus, 1929 is the twelfth year of the one hundred and twenty-eighth indiction after Christ.

the most reverend Pope Gregory and of our King and Queen
and of all the nobles of the entire realm of England, to which
end I have not delayed to do; so, with the consent and approval of all our clergy, I do accordingly liberate and exempt
it from all episcopal rule, subjection and disturbance; and to
all those who shall have longed to visit and shall have visited
that church, with alms and offerings, we do remit a third part
of their penance. And that this may remain for ever unshaken,
unchanged and also inviolable, by the authority of the Father
Son and Holy Ghost we forbid all our successors from presuming to attempt anything contrary to this decree.

That the Mount was much frequented by pilgrims in
the fifteenth century is unquestionable. In 1472 when
John de Vere, Earl of Oxford, and his followers entered
the Mount it is said that they entered as pilgrims.
The Compotus Roll of 1482 refers to the shrine of
St Michael; in fact, the first source of income to be
mentioned in it is that derived from certain oblations
in gold and silver offered before the image of St
Michael. Elsewhere in the same document we read
that the Earl of Oxford (or his companions) had
seized money amounting to £10 out of the chest
which contained the offerings.

William of Worcester, writing in 1478, gives a
slightly altered version of the above quoted charter,
a translation of which is here inserted for the sake of
comparison:

"To all (those) of holy mother the church who shall read
or hear the present letter, greeting. Be it known unto you all
that the most holy Pope Gregory in the year of the Lord's in-

carnation 1070, from the love and very great devotion which he bore towards the church of St Michael's Mount, in Tumba, in the county of Cornwall, piously granted to the church aforesaid which is believed and acknowledged to be consecrated and sanctified by the ministry of angels, (and) to all the faithful who should seek the welfare of that church or visit it with alms and offerings, the remission of one third part of their penance. And that this (grant) should ever remain unshaken and inviolable, by the authority of God the Father Almighty and the Son and Holy Spirit he forbad all his successors from presuming to attempt anything contrary to this decree". These very words found in the old registers, discovered afresh in this church, are accordingly placed here publicly on the doors of the church. And inasmuch as this matter is unknown to many, therefore we, in Christ, the servants of God and ministers of this church, require and beg all of you who have the direction of souls, for the spreading of the news one to another, to publish those words in your churches in order that those who are under your rule and control may be the more earnestly roused to greater eagerness in devotion and by pilgrimage frequent that place in greater splendour, (offer) the gifts and graciously obtain the indulgences.

It will be observed that Bishop Leofric's name does not occur in the translation and that Pope Gregory's grant is dated 1070, that is, three years before he became pope. It must be left to the reader to solve these problems. The object sought by the publication of the charter was admittedly to encourage pilgrimages. From this time until the suppression of the monastery of Syon the shrine of St Michael drew large numbers of pilgrims. Norden writing in 1584 states that the Mount "hath bene muche resorted unto by Pylgrims in devotion to St Michaell whose chayre is fabled to be in the Mount on the south syde of verie Daungerous access". Norden may have had personal knowledge of the facts, but the expression "fabled to be" would rather imply that he got his information at second hand. Consequently too much reliance must not be placed upon his statement respecting the "chayre".

About the time of the suppression, in 1538 to be exact, William Williams, a fletcher of Salisbury, Richard Hussey, chaplain, Thomas Selman, singing-man, and Philip Godfray, tailor, were summoned before the Mayor of Salisbury and other commissioners in respect of a report that an angel had appeared to the king then at Portsmouth and had bidden him go on pilgrimage to St Michael's Mount and offer a noble there on pain of death, and according to Jane Delond, widow, that Queen Jane (Seymour) had appeared to him and desired him to go on the same pilgrimage. The evidence given before the commission is very conflicting.[1] Jane Delond said she heard it of four neighbours whose names are given: Godfray heard it of John Higgins of Durneford. The evidence of John Hawkes, smith, stated that Isabel Nowell of Sarum, widow, came to his house to fetch fire and said, "God save the King, I trust we shall go on pilgrimage again for I hear say that his Grace will go on pilgrimage to St Michael's Mount", and Nowell

---

[1] See State Papers, 10, Aug. 1538.

when questioned not only did not deny the imputa-
tion but added that "an angel did appear to his
Grace for the same", giving as her authority one
Agnes, wife of John Chacy.

The charge was trivial enough and the evidence
worthy of it. Incidentally we learn that pilgrimages
to the Mount were very widely known and that
Widow Nowell had pleasant recollections of them.

It is necessary to add something concerning the
shrine of St Michael. Was it inside the chapel or
without? Norden's statement would lead us to distinguish between the shrine and the chair. Whether
the chair was near the south-west pinnacle of the
tower or in the south of the Mount itself there would
be difficulties, in the matter of access and of participation in the religious ceremonial, which would be
practically insurmountable. In an inventory taken in
the first half of the sixteenth century[1] preserved in
the Public Record Office will be found *inter alia* an
image of St Michael of silver and gilt, two bonnets
for St Michael and a chain of gold also a bawderyk
(? hauberk, i.e. coat of mail), silver and gilt for St
Michael. The coats and bonnets are described as
costly, and therefore can hardly be regarded as
coverings for the protection of the image when it was
not required. A coat of mail, in fact the entire
panoply of war, is quite in keeping with traditional
representatives of the archangel who, but for his
wings, may easily be mistaken for St George, but the

[1] For this inventory see p. 80. The P.R.O. reference is Q.R.
E. 117.

bonnet is unusual though Raphael is said to have designed a St Michael wearing a helmet. The bonnet may have been something like an amice made to be thrown back so as to form a collar round the neck.[1] In Italian art generally nothing is more characteristic of St Michael than the open brow and the long flowing hair caught by the breeze caused by the swiftness of his flight. To quote a modern writer

who indeed can forbear to remember him whom Perugino painted—him who stands young, ruddy, strong and triumphant, girt with shining armour, belted and greaved, yet swift, ready and at ease, with free, uncovered face and the wind moving in his hair as he waits with hand upon sword and shield, in the pause between task and task, poised at rest in the evening stillness, before another day dawn and his labours begin anew.[2]

[1] In the Sithney Inventory of Church Goods (1553–8) there occurs a "bonnet of blewe sylke".

[2] H. S. Holland, *Logic and Life*, p. 262. All such representations, whether of St Michael or St George, are, of course, based upon St Paul's description of the Christian warrior—Ephesians vi. 13–17.

The Corody at the Mount

A CORODY (*conredia*) was equivalent to a right of hospitality in a religious house. The right was heritable. The founder or benefactor of a monastery might reserve a corody for himself and his successors which entitled him or them to nominate a person to enjoy the hospitality of the house he had endowed. Or he might purchase a corody for himself. Life in a monastery under these circumstances could hardly fail to be attractive to men who had served their king and country, and had nothing further to look forward to save a solitary and necessitous old age. It has even been suggested that the prospect of generous fare, dignified leisure and genial companionship appealed to some who were at a loose end. In any case the fellowship of cultured men who, during the intervals allowed between the performance of their several religious duties, studied music, philosophy, architecture, painting, or who devoted themselves to agriculture and gardening, would be a welcome refuge to the disappointed and friendless wayfarer. The origin of the corody "issuing out of" St Michael's Mount is obscure, and the problem is complicated owing to the fact that the king at a comparatively early period claimed the right to corodies in those monasteries of royal foundation even where no such right had been reserved. An example will make this clear. In 1346 King Edward III requested Randolf, Abbot of Dieulacres in Staffordshire, to receive

Richard de Preston into his abbey. The abbot refused
on the ground that he held his house and lands not of
the king but as of the honour and sword of Chester,
and that Ranulph, Earl of Chester, was the founder
of the abbey. The jury found that such was the case
and gave a verdict for the abbot. In the case of St
Michael's Mount the king frequently bestowed the
corody, but there is no evidence to show that he did
so because Edward the Confessor was the reputed
founder of the priory. Moreover, there is no pretext
advanced—as was so frequently the case in the be-
stowal of the priory's patronage—that it was owing
to the wars with France. And yet throughout a
lengthened period the family of Trevarthian claimed
to be the patrons of the corody and based their claim
upon their surrender of the advowson of St Hilary in
exchange for the corody. The following extracts from
the Patent Rolls and the *Cartulary* will serve by way
of illustration.

In 1323 Alfonsus de Ispannia, who had long
served the king, was sent to the prior and convent of
St Michael's Mount to receive the same maintenance
as Alan Dannek had in his lifetime at the king's
request.[1]

In 1334 at the king's request the prior, Peter Car-
ville (*de Cara Villa*), and his brethren admitted Roland Trewinnard into the priory and granted to him
for life his reasonable estover in eatables and drink-
ables, gown, chamber and half a mark for shoe
leather, the said Roland to have 18*s.* instead of a

[1] Pat. Rolls, 1323.

gown if he preferred it. John Trevarthian was one of the witnesses.[1]

In 1337 the king granted to his squire, John Meisy, the maintenance which John Trevardian (Trevarthian) lately held in the priory by grant of the late prior "which is in the King's gift by reason of the forfeiture incurred by the said Trevardian".[2]

We are not told what Trevarthian had done to forfeit his corody and the *Cartulary* does not record Meisy's admission. It looks as if the King's advisers had mistaken the patronage of the corody for the corody itself, and this conjecture is rendered probable by reason of certain proceedings taken by Trevarthian in the king's court two years later and recorded in the *Cartulary*. Trevarthian states that he has demanded of the prior suitable daily maintenance for himself and his heirs and a garcion and horse; also during four days, viz. at the Feasts of Christmas, Easter, Whitsuntide and All Saints, maintenance in victuals for four men of his tenantry with serving men and four horses, four greyhounds and four sparrow hawks, or in default immediate possession of the advowson of St Hilary of which he states his predecessor has been disseised by the prior's predecessor in exchange for the said profits. To put an end to all further dispute he is prepared to accept suitable maintenance for himself (or nominee) and a garcion and horse with all necessaries suitable for a squire, and on these conditions quit-claims the advowson to the prior.[3]

[1] *Cartulary*.   [2] Pat. Rolls, 1337.   [3] *Cartulary*.

In the year 1347 the Prior of St Michael's admitted Roger Copper, a nominee of the king, to the priory, "to have the same as Roland Trewinnard had". A few days later, in the same year, the said Roger executed a deed by which, on the payment of a sum of money to him by the prior, he resigns the corody and by an indenture dated September 28th agrees to protect the priory against all claims touching the same. The sum paid to him by the prior was £30 in two instalments, and the receipts for the money are entered in the *Cartulary*.

The claim of the Trevarthians was not surrendered, for at the inquest held after the death of Joan Hulle in 1429 it was found that as the relict of Sir John Trevarthian she had held, as dower, "a certain corody issuing out of St Michael's Mount".

The suppression of the alien priories by Henry V and the grant of St Michael's Mount to the Abbess and Sisters of Syon probably abolished the corody, although it is explicitly stated in Edward IV's confirmation of the grant in 1461 that all chantries and advowsons heretofore belonging to the priory are to remain to the said abbess,[1] and if the abbess got the advowson of St Hilary which had been given by the Trevarthians to the priory in exchange for the corody, what did the Trevarthians get as the result of the suppression of corody?

[1] Pat. Rolls, 1 Edward IV.

Military and Civil

THE spear-heads, battle-axes and swords of copper found at the foot of the Mount in the sixteenth century as related by Camden may carry us back to a time when Ictis was exporting tin to the Mediterranean, when the tin-store required to be guarded against enemies, native or foreign. At a much later period the Mount must have struck the observer as being a naturally impregnable fortress. When Edward the Confessor gave or confirmed it to the monks his thoughts were not of this world's warriors but of those who led a high and heavenly life.

Henry de la Pomeray, however, saw its possibilities as a military outpost. Through his wife he had become possessed of the manor of Roseworthy which, like many other manors, reckoned among its members lands outside its own boundary, and among them Trengwainton and Landithy. The church of St Madron was known as St Madern de Rudwori (Roseworthy). It is therefore reasonable to conclude that Pomeray, whose Cornish seat was at Tregony, knew the neighbourhood, and the natural strength of the fortress of St Michael's Mount.

At the time of the Domesday Survey Radulphus de Pomaria was one of the largest landowners in the county of Devon. His grandson (or great-grandson), Henry,[1] married Rohesia, sister of Reginald, Earl of

[1] Sir William Pole, *Description of Devon*, p. 281; Vivian, *Visit*, p. 380.

Cornwall, who between the years 1159 and 1173 gave to her and her heirs the manor of Roseworthy, to hold of him and his heirs.[1] Reginald died without heirs of his body, and the manor thereupon came to be held by the Pomerays as tenants in chief.

In the year 1189 Richard I, when about to set forth on the great crusade, gave the county of Cornwall to his brother John of infamous memory. Four years later, while Richard was a prisoner in the hands of the emperor, John attempted to seize the crown, and Henry de la Pomeray on his behalf occupied St Michael's Mount. He expelled the monks and fortified it. He was accompanied by Jollan, his only son by his wife Rohesia. Hoveden gives a succinct but valuable account of both father and son.[2] Of Henry he says: "St Michael's Mount which Henry de la Pomeray, having expelled the monks, had fortified against the King was surrendered to the Archbishop" (who was in command of the king's forces). "Henry indeed having heard of the King's arrival died of fright" (*timore perterritus*). Of Jollan he says: "On the morrow of Coronation day, Jollan brother of Henry de la Pomerai (the son and heir of the abovementioned Henry by his first wife, Matilda de Vitrei) who was summoned because he had most treacherously (*proditiose*) been present at the capture of St Michael's Mount, preferred rather to be exiled from England than to stand his trial in the King's Court".

---

[1] The charter is among the muniments at Tregothnan and a full account of it is given in the *Journ. Roy. Inst. of Cornwall*, 1864.

[2] Hoveden, III, 6. Pipe Rolls, 6 Richard I.

The Pipe Roll of Michaelmas 1194 records the payments of fines by eight men who were in the Mount against the king. The fines are of small amount. Of the rebels, one was a smith and three were carpenters. One described as the son of Dodde of Lismanoch, paid 8*s*. 4*d*. Henry de la Pomeray the son, however, was required to pay 700 marks and Robert de Vitrei was one of the thirteen bondsmen.

POMERAY

Or a lion gules in a border engrailed sable

On the death of Richard I John succeeded to the crown. His character—a complex of vices—is well known. We learn from a Pipe Roll[1] of 1204 "that when Henry de la Pomeray, the son of Henry, applied to have such seisin of the land of Roseworthy as his father had on the day he entered the castle of Mount St Michael, for which he had been disseised of that land, he was required to pay the then large sum of sixty marks".

The second Henry de la Pomeray appears to have made Tregony Castle, which he is said to have built, his place of residence. A very vivid illustration of the social life of the period is supplied by an Assize Roll of the year 1213. To paraphrase it would be to spoil it:

At the sheriff's hundred court at Treuueru (Truro) Baldwin Tyrel complained that Henry de Pomeray and Alan

[1] Pipe Rolls, 6 John, m. 4.

de Dunstanville imprisoned him in chains at Tregeny in the lowest cell of H. de Pomereia and tried to extort money. Failing that they took him in the middle of the night into the town of Tregeny and raised the hue and cry (*cornaverunt huces*) and handed him over to the burgesses. The sergeant of the hundred of Penrethair (Penwith) found him imprisoned and arranged for his release. Alan de Dunstanville declared that he had sent his steward Roger de Lancuc (Nancekuke) to take possession of a fee which Harry de Heligan, who had just died held of him, and that he found the house (Baldwin's) fortified and barricaded (*castellata et bretachiata*) and Baldwin, fully armed, resisted his entrance and declared that the King had been murdered in North Wales. Roger the steward, however, does not bear this out but says he was refused entrance by Henerie lord of that fee who denied the right of such seisin as he was of age. Henry de Pomeray says that he and Alan were together in his house at Tregeni on the day of St Leonard, and so were spending a merry evening together (*sic fuerunt hilares simul in sero*). A servant warned him of a suspicious man lurking about with a bow and arrows and when he went up to bed preceded by a man carrying a candle, an arrow suddenly flew past the hand of the man with the candle and going out they caught Baldwin with his bow. This again is not borne out.

We are not told the result of this enquiry. Before leaving the Pomerays it may be interesting to add that as lord of Roseworthy of which Trengwainton was a member, the first Henry de la Pomeray gave the advowson of Madron to the Prior of the Knights Hospitallers, but the royal assent had not been obtained at the time of his death. In the year 1204 the forfeited lands were restored to his son, the second Henry. Thereupon the prior sought the ratification of the grant and the matter upon being referred to twelve men of Roseworthy, they reported on oath that the first Henry had given the advowson to the prior and that it rightly belonged to him. King John confirmed this grant to the prior by charter in 1206.

The next reference (we have met with) to the fortress of St Michael's Mount is in 1338, a few months before Edward I invaded France. In that year Ralph Bloyou, the last hope of the Breton family of that name upon which the Conqueror had conferred seven fees in the county of Cornwall, was required to relinquish the custody of the fortlet then in the king's hands, together with other possessions of the prior. In his stead Reginald de Boterels (Botreaux) and John Hamly, Sheriff of Cornwall, were appointed. Reginald de Botreaux had been summoned in 1324 to attend the Great Council at Westminster, and in the same year appointed joint guardian together with Richard Beaupré, Rector of St Just, of the alien priories of Cornwall. It is clear that Bloyou's removal implied no lack of confidence, for in the same year he was appointed a commissioner of array and a justice of oyer and terminer. Ralph Bloyou was the last male representative of a family which for well nigh three centuries had occupied a prominent position, not only in West Cornwall but in the hundred of Trigg, but the immediate progenitors of Ralph had been distinguished by their lawlessness rather than by their public services.

Ralph Bloyou was born at Truthwall on the Monday after the Nativity of the Blessed Virgin 1296, and baptised the following day "in the Church of St Ludevon in that vill". He had a licence from the bishop for the celebration of Divine Service in his chapel of St Electa (Elette) in Endellion parish in 1331, and four years later he had the king's licence to crenellate his mansion at Truthwall (Tregewel) in Ludgvan and at Coleweheys in the county of Dorset. No trace of the former place of residence now exists. It was probably situated at or near the site of the great mine known in the eighteenth century as Wheal Fortune. As a justice of assize Sir Ralph Bloyou encountered the popular opposition for which Cornwall was notorious. On his way to Lostwithiel in the year 1338, in pursuance of his commission, "certain disturbers of the peace, of malice aforethought, as he came to Glyn, assaulted him and followed him thence with armed force, carried away his goods, assaulted his men and servants and prevented him from executing his office".[1] Two commissions of enquiry were appointed, and in the second of these (in 1340) John Lercedekne and Henry de Erch were specifically charged as leaders of the mob, from which it may be inferred that personal malice or jealousy was at the root of the assault. It is, however, remarkable that in the same year we find in a confirmation of a charter granted by Edward the Black Prince, respecting the court of fees and the court of gate (*court des fedz & court de Geyte*) at Launceston, Monsieur Rauf de

[1] Pat. Rolls, 12 and 14 Edward III.

Bloyou, Monsieur Johan Lercedekne and Monsieur Johan Petit acting together on a commission appointed to determine whether the former court was of recent or of ancient origin. We do not know the date of Sir Ralph Bloyou's death. It is certain, however, that he died without issue and that his lands passed to his two sisters, Elizabeth and Joan. From the former are descended the Boscawens, Pole Carews and Prideaux Brunes.

It will have been observed that the aforenamed governors of the Mount were appointed by the king in the time of war. In times of peace there were presumably bailiffs only, whose business it was to collect the customs of the port. The charter of Edward the Confessor had given to St Michael for the use of the brothers serving God in the same place, St Michael which is near the sea with all appurtenances, to wit vills, lands, castles and all thereunto belonging, and Count Robert of Mortain had, with the Conqueror's assent, also given the Mount to the monks, freedom from outside legal jurisdiction, save in cases of homicide only. It is clear that so long as Normandy remained subject to the English king little danger was to be apprehended from either the Norman or Cornish monastery and their occupants. They were both equally the king's subjects, instinct with the same sense of loyalty. When in the reign of King John, Normandy ceased to acknowledge the King of England as sovereign the case was entirely altered. The problem to be solved was—to whom did the monks owe allegiance? And the problem had been rendered the more difficult of solution owing to the conditions formulated in 1135 when the priory of St Michael of Cornwall was formally constituted and the priory church consecrated by Robert Chichester, Bishop of Exeter. In the charter of constitution it is enacted that the Cornish brethren shall receive the benediction of the monastic order at the hands of the Abbot of Mont St Michel and that if the Prior of St Michael's Mount prove refractory he shall be degraded and another prior appointed by the abbot. A Norman abbot having thus acquired almost complete control over the priory and its monks it would have been surprising if the King of England had not taken every precaution against treachery on the part of the abbot's nominees. Theoretically a monk might recognise no country as his own save Christendom: but practically, to his credit be it said, he never ceased to be a Norman or an Englishman as the case might be. On this account we are prepared for the injunctions issued in 1342 to the bailiffs to make diligent scrutiny of all who leave the port and to seize all letters they consider suspect and send them into chancery; the king having learned that there are spies who forewarn the king's enemies.[1] We are also prepared for the compulsory surrender of the priory into the king's hands in the time of war. Such surrenders were frequent and included the patronage of all churches belonging to it and the appointment of the prior in the event of the priory becoming vacant. In 1385 Richard II appointed Richard Auncell,

---

[1] Pat. Rolls, 16 Edward III, Mar. 20th.

monk, of Tavistock, to the priory when he was at war with France.

The allegiance which the monks of St Michael's Mount owed to the Abbot of Mont St Michel, as specified in the *Constructio* of the former in 1135, had become considerably moderated in so far as it was temporal and secular when, in 1356, John Hardy, Prior of St Michael's Mount, was accused of treasonable conduct. The terms of the *Constructio* required a yearly payment of sixteen marks by the prior to the abbot, and the charge against Prior Hardy was that he had sent by his brother secret letters and sums amounting to £60 into Normandy to the king's enemies and had also harboured two men of that country for two weeks at his manor of Treverabo. The prior was able to prove his innocence and acquitted.

War with France, beginning with Edward the Third's invasion of that country in 1339, continued with brief interruptions for over a century and was fraught with disaster to the priory as a Benedictine convent. It is moreover noteworthy that during that period we hear nothing of the Mount as a military outpost or as a naval base. The thought of England's invasion was never entertained for a single moment. Not until the seizure of the Mount by the Earl of Oxford in the year 1472, when the use of explosives was in process of introduction, does the provision of a garrison appear to have been considered necessary.

John de Vere, Earl of Oxford

THE rival claims of the houses of York and Lancaster to the English crown were based in either case upon hereditary right of succession. The deposition of Richard II, and the recognition of Henry IV as his successor, was a violation of this principle; for, assuming hereditary right to have been at that time the governing principle, Edmund, Earl of March, was the rightful heir to the throne. Edmund was descended from Lionel, Duke of Clarence, the third son of Edward III, whereas Henry, who succeeded to the crown in the year 1399 as Henry IV, was descended from John of Gaunt, the fourth son. The Earl of March was, at the time, only a child and died in 1424. His sister Anne married Richard, Earl of Cambridge, and became the mother of Richard, Duke of York. On the death of Henry IV his son Henry V was acclaimed king, and by his noble qualities and heroism worthily upheld the best traditions of a royal race. His son Henry was an infant at the time of his death, and was neither physically nor mentally fitted to cope with the ambitious designs of the powerful nobles who surrounded him. All might have gone well with him had not the loss of the conquered French provinces, the huge debt incurred by his ministers, and the consequent burdens imposed upon his subjects, created discontent throughout the kingdom. His queen—Margaret of Anjou—brave, beautiful and accomplished, did all that was, humanly speaking, possible to uphold the throne; and it was not until she gave birth to a son in 1454, which augured a continuance of the house of Lancaster, that Richard, Duke of York, asserted his claim to the crown. Under colour of reforming the government he levied war against the king, and in 1455 the battle of St Albans was fought in which he was successful. Thus commenced the Wars of the Roses, which lasted thirty years. At the battle of Wakefield in 1460 he was slain, and his son Edward —afterwards Edward IV, was left to uphold the Yorkist claim. He was declared king by the citizens of London in the following year. Meanwhile the war continued with varying success and failure until 1471, when the Lancastrians were finally defeated on May 4th at the battle of Tewkesbury. Queen Margaret and her son were captured. The queen was thrown into the Tower and her son brutally murdered. King Henry died in that confinement a few days later. Of the Lancastrians no one had exhibited greater devotion or greater courage than John de Vere, Earl of Oxford.

John de Vere, the thirteenth earl, was the second son of John, the twelfth earl, and grandson of Richard, the eleventh earl, who married Alice, one of the daughters and co-heiresses of Sir Richard Sergeaux, and widow of Guy St Aubyn. John, the twelfth earl, whose late arrival at the battle of St Albans 1455 had aroused suspicion in regard to his political leanings, was arrested together with Aubrey, his eldest son, in 1461, on a charge of arranging for a Lancastrian landing on the east coast, and condemned to death by the constable's court, and executed on Tower Hill on February 24th, 1462. Aubrey de Vere left no issue, and his brother John, with whom we are concerned, became thirteenth earl. He was thrown into the Tower on suspicion in 1468 but was released soon afterwards. At a later date, as constable, he had the satisfaction of passing sentence of death upon John Tiptoft, who, in that capacity, had condemned his father and brother. He fought at Barnet in 1471 (April 14th) where the Lancastrians were totally defeated. The earl escaped to France. Shakespeare is lavish in his praises of the earl, and represents him as present at the battle of Tewkesbury. In a supposed conversation between him and the Earl of Warwick (at that time a supporter of the Yorkish claim) the poet no doubt expresses the popular estimate of the Earl of Oxford.

VERE, EARL OF
OXFORD

Quarterly gules and or with a molet argent in the quarter

Warwick.	Can Oxford, that did ever fence the right,
	Now buckler falsehood with a pedigree?
	For shame! leave Henry, and call Edward King.
Oxford.	Call him my king, by whose injurious doom
	My elder brother, the Lord Aubrey Vere,
	Was done to death? and more than so, my father,

Even in the downfall of his mellow'd years,
When nature brought him to the door of death?
No, Warwick, no; while life upholds this arm,
This arm upholds the house of Lancaster.

And elsewhere Warwick speaks of him as "brave Oxford, wondrous well belov'd".

There is no reliable evidence that he was present at the battle of Tewkesbury. Upon his arrival at Dieppe, after the battle of Barnet, he proceeded to fit out a small squadron, some say of eighty and some say 397 men, and with them, having proved their mettle by successful privateering, on September 30th he landed with his brothers Thomas and George at St Michael's Mount, and with his men disguised as pilgrims entered and took possession. Warkworth's account of the Mount and its siege by the king's forces is of great interest and is here given at large.[1]

Also in the 13th year of the reign of King Edward, Sir John Veer, Earl of Oxford, that withdrew him(self) from Barnet field and rode into Scotland, and from thence into France, sailed, and there he was worshipfully received. And in the same year he was in the sea with certain ships, and got great good(s) and riches, and afterwards came into West Country,

---

[1] John Warkworth, D.D., Master of St Peter's College, Cambridge, was a contemporary who died in the year 1500. He wrote a *Chronicle of the first thirteen years of the Reign of King Edward the Fourth*. The text of this work was published from the manuscript preserved at Peterhouse, by the Camden Society in 1839. At Peterhouse will be found also a portrait of the writer. In the above extract from the *Chronicle* the present writer has taken the liberty of presenting it in modern spelling while retaining the syntax of the original.

and with a subtle point of war, got and entered Saint Michael's Mount in Cornwall, a strong place and a mighty, and can not be got, if it be well victualled with a few men to keep it; for 20 men may keep it against all the world. So the said Earl with 20 score men save three, the last day of September the year afore said entered first into the said Mount, and he and his men came down into (the) county of Cornwall and had right good cheer of the commons etc. The King and his Council saw that thereof much harm might grow and commanded Bodrygan, Sheriff ruler of Cornwall, to besiege the said Mount. And so he did; and every day the Earl of Oxford's men came down under truce, spake with Bodrygan and his men; and at the last the said Earl lacked victual, and the said Bodrygan suffered him to be victualled; and anon the King was put in knowledge thereof; wherefore the said Bodrygan was discharged, and Richard Fortescu, squire for the body, by authority of the King took upon hand to lay siege to the aforesaid Mount. And so great divisions arose betwixt Bodrygan and Fortescu, which Fortescu was sheriff of Cornwall; and the said Fortescu laid siege the 23rd day of December the year aforesaid; and for the most part every day each of them fought with other, and the said Earl's men killed divers of Fortescu's men; and some times when they had well fought they would take a truce for one day and a night and sometimes for two or three days. In the which truces each one of them spake and communed with other. The King and his Council sent unto divers that were with the Earl of Oxford privily their pardons, and promised to them great gifts and lands and goods, by the which divers of them were turned to the King against the Earl; and so in conclusion the Earl had not passing 8 or 9 men that would hold with him; the which was the undoing of the Earl. For there is a proverb and a

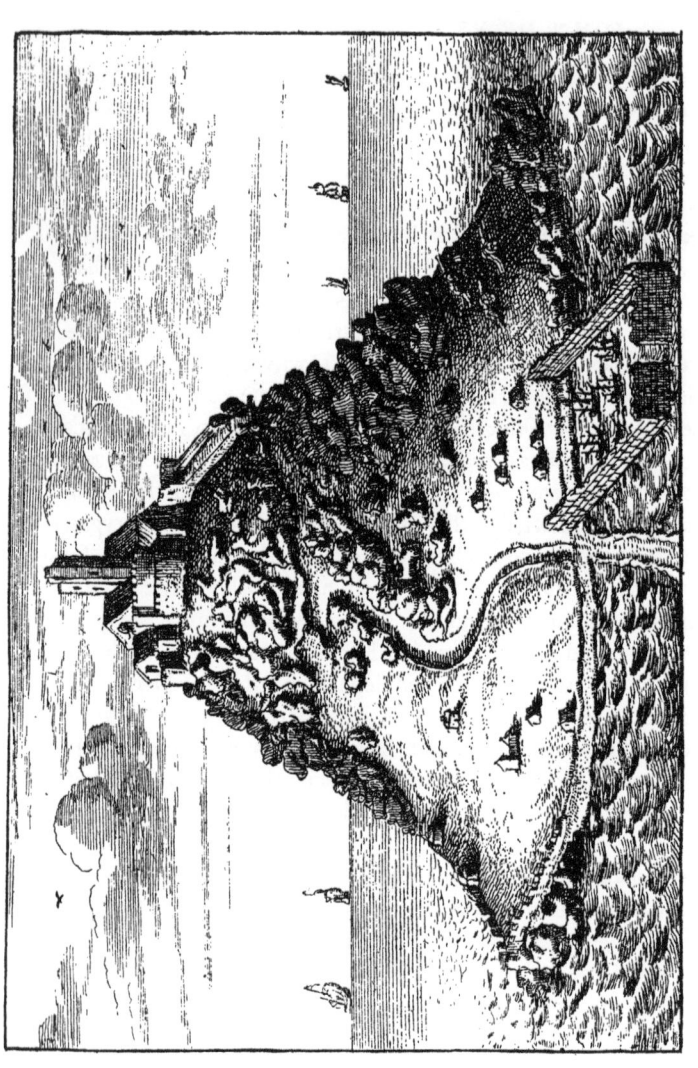

ST MICHAEL'S MOUNT IN 1582

(Norden: Speculi Britanniae)

saying that *a castle that speaketh and a woman that will hear, they will be gotten both*: for men that being in a castle of war that will speak and entreat with their enemies, the conclusion thereof (is) the losing of the castle; and a woman that will hear folly spoken unto her, if she assent not at one time, she will at another. And as this proverb was proved true by the said Earl of Oxford which was fain to yield up the said Mount and put him in the King's grace; if he had not done so, his own men would have brought him out. And so Fortescu entered into the said Mount the 15th day of February the year aforesaid, in the which was victual enough till Midsummer after. And so was the Earl aforesaid, the Lord Bemonde, two brothers of the said Earl, and Thomas Clyfforde brought as a prisoner to the King; and all was done by their own folly.

The siege of the Mount was certainly one of the most remarkable recorded in history. The authenticity of the main facts recorded by John Warkworth is beyond question. William of Worcester writing, as he is careful to point out, within five years of the event, tells us that John de Vere, Earl of Oxford, entered St Michael's Mount on the morrow of Michaelmas 1473 with a total force of eighty followers and withstood a siege for twenty-six weeks against the king's army of six thousand fighting men. The following extracts from the public records afford strong evidence of the truth of the above statements. When the king learnt that de Vere was in possession of the Mount he lost no time in attempting its recapture. On October 27th he issued a commission[1] to John Arundell, knight; John Colshyll, knight; John

[1] Pat. Rolls of the above date.

Crocker, knight, John Fortescu, Henry Bodrugan, John Sturgeon, Thomas Whalesburgh, John Trenoweth, Thomas Trefrye, John Arundell, John Tremayne, John Carmynowe, Richard Eggescombe, John Devyok, Oliver Wise, Edward Assheton, John Pentire, John Moile, William Tavenour, John Penpons, John Wydeslade the younger, and William Horde to array the king's liege of the county of Cornwall and of other counties adjacent if necessary, to conquer John, late Earl of Oxford, and other rebels who have entered St Michael's Mount, Co. Cornwall, and to bring back the Mount into the king's hands and provide for its safe custody and defence.

On November 20th the king entered into a covenant with Captain William Featherstone of the *Caragon*, Captain Edward Brampton of the *Garce* and Captain Thomas Batson of the *Cristofore* of Calais who were instructed, Featherstone with 260 men, Brampton with 200 men and Batson with 75 men, "to be about the basement of St Michael's Mount for two months and afterwards and, until the said place begotten or yelden to the King's obedience, they shall continually attend upon the said siege".[1]

On December 7th a further commission[2] was issued to John Fortescue, one of the esquires of the body, Sheriff of Cornwall, John Crokker, knight, and Henry Bodrugan, Esq., giving full power and authority to reduce St Michael's Mount to the king's

---

[1] Cott. MSS. xvii, 19. Cf. Pat. Rolls of same date.
[2] Pat. Rolls, 13 Edward IV, Dec. 7th, 1473.

obedience and place it under secure custody and governance and conquer John, late Earl of Oxford, and others who have entered the Mount, and hold it as a refuge, and make excursions to the adjoining parts; and to promise pardon to any rebels within the Mount who may be willing to submit and take an oath of fealty, with the exception of the said earl, William Beaumond late Lord Bardolf Knight, and George Veer, Thomas Veer, and Richard Veer, brothers of the earl.

Six days later Richard Patyn and Richard Veron were appointed[1] to take carriage by land and sea and fresh water for divers ordnance which the king has ordered to be taken to St Michael's Mount against the rebels there, and timber and iron and other necessaries for the same, and carpenters called "whelewrights" and "cartwrights" and other carpenters.

Notwithstanding the truces, referred to by Warkworth, and the exchange of civilities between the opposing armies, the above extracts from authoritative documents make it sufficiently clear that both attackers and attacked were in deadly earnest. In one particular Warkworth appears to have been in error. Henry Bodrugan was not discharged. His name appears in both commissions issued for the conquest and capture of the earl. Moreover, as Mr W. J. Blake[2] has pointed out, when he was attainted on a charge of treason in the following year no mention is

[1] Pat. Rolls, 13 Edward IV, Dec. 13th, 1473.
[2] *Journ. Roy. Inst. of Cornwall*, xx.

made of his aiding or abetting the earl. Bodrugan was probably the most turbulent and most powerful, and also in some respects the most unscrupulous man in Cornwall, but to the end he remained true to the House of York.

The first name in the Commission of Array of October 26th, 1473, is that of Sir John Arundell. Many members of the several branches of the Arundell family have borne the name of John, and many of those who were so named in their baptism have received the accolade of knighthood. This Sir John Arundell was of Trerice, and served as sheriff of the county in 1471. By the marriage of his grandfather to the heiress of John Durant, esquire, the manor of Ebbingford on the shores of Bude Bay had passed to the Arundells, who made it their principal place of residence. Sir John—so the story runs—had, in the exercise of his functions as magistrate, sentenced an offender to imprisonment, who in true Cornish fashion had "ill wished" him and foretold a day

> When upon the yellow sand
> Thou shalt die by human hand.

Thereupon Sir John had removed from Ebbingford to Trerice, a mansion and manor in Newlyn parish, which had been acquired by the Arundells in the reign of King Edward III and which was judged sufficiently remote from the "yellow sand" to break the spell of the prophetic utterance. But alas! all was in vain.

In a sally of Lord Oxford's men the worthy knight

was slain on the yellow sand of Mount's Bay. Richard Carew, who relates the story, states that he was buried in the chapel of St Michael's Mount.

On February 15th, 1473, Lord Oxford surrendered, and together with his two brothers was captured. Attainted and imprisoned in Hamme Castle near Calais his courage remained undaunted. After three years' imprisonment he contrived to escape, and joined Henry, Earl of Richmond, in Paris. With him he invaded England in 1485 and as captain-general had command of the right wing of Richmond's army at the battle of Bosworth, where Richard III was slain. Upon Richmond's accession to the throne as Henry VII, Oxford's career was assured. King Henry had an excellent memory. Oxford's attainder was reversed. Office and honours were freely bestowed upon him. Henry appointed him one of the executors of his will. He was also one of the sponsors of Henry VIII. When the Cornish rebels came up to London in the summer of 1497, led by Michael Joseph, the smith of St Keverne, Thomas Flamank, a lawyer of Bodmin, and Lord Audley who refused to pay the subsidies levied in that year, it was the Earl of Oxford who cut off their retreat. The earl died in the year 1513. His second wife was the widow of William Viscount Beaumont who, as we have seen, was Oxford's companion at the Mount in 1473. He left no issue, and his honours and dignities passed to his nephew, the fourteenth earl.

It does not appear that Warkworth, whose delightful description of the siege of the Mount has been given above, fully grasped the strenuousness of the struggle which took place. A glance at the Compotus Roll of 1482 presented by Vivian Treonney, deputy of John Fortescue, esquire, and receiver for the Lady Abbess of Syon, includes a claim for £10 taken out of the alms box, £60 for damage done to the house by fire and destruction, £56. 5s. 5d. for damage done by the king's forces, and £4 for damage done by John Penpons, esquire. There are also claims for the maintenance of detachments of soldiers on three several occasions, also for sixteen shillings worth of gunpowder and ten shillings worth of brimstone for the purpose of making gunpowder. A gift to Henry Langston who chanced to be at the Mount during the siege for counsel and advice is included. It is manifest therefore that the abbess was under no obligation to provide for the Mount's defence and that Henry VII, whose foresight was only equalled by his diligence in procuring evidence of the loyalty or otherwise of his subjects, was totally unprepared for the third occupation of the Mount in the year 1497.

A hundred and twenty pounds in the fifteenth century was a large sum, and to inflict so much damage with the artillery of the period upon a castle, to use Warkworth's words, "so strong and mighty", proves that the siege was a serious affair to those who took part in it. No doubt when fortune smiled upon the Earl of Oxford—"brave Oxford, wondrous well belov'd"—he made ample recompense for the loan of the £10 taken from the alms box.

Perkin Warbeck

KING Edward IV died rather suddenly on April 9th, 1483, having on his death-bed appointed his brother Richard, Duke of Gloucester, to be regent during his son's minority. The king left two sons, Edward, then in his twelfth year, who succeeded to the crown, and Richard, Duke of York, in his ninth year. The male representatives of the House of York thus consisted of the two aforesaid royal princes, Edward, Earl of Warwick, a boy of ten years, son of George, Duke of Clarence, and their uncle, the said Richard.

On June 26th, Richard usurped the crown and caused the two young princes, Edward and Richard, to be murdered in the Tower. The secrecy with which this crime was accomplished left room for doubts of which advantage was to be taken later on.

Richard's reign was of short duration. He was killed at the battle of Bosworth on August 22nd, 1485.

At this time the two men of greatest influence in the county of Cornwall were Sir Henry Bodrugan and Sir Richard Edgcombe, the former Yorkist and the latter Lancastrian. Both fought at Bosworth. Bodrugan escaped and sought concealment; Edgcombe was knighted on the field, admitted to King Henry's privy council and became one of the king's most valued advisers.

As a precautionary measure Henry committed to the Tower Edward, Earl of Warwick, and rumours

were soon afloat that he had shared the fate of his two
cousins. These rumours must have been widespread
and generally believed, or the attempt to foist a
joiner's son, Lambert Simnel by name, upon the
throne would never have been made. The Oxford
priest who trained this youth to play the rôle of prince
evidently believed Warwick to be dead, and it is
probable that Lincoln, Broughton and Bodrugan,
who espoused his cause, believed him to be alive. Be
that as it may, the real motive which lay behind this
and other attempts to unseat Henry, was that of the
old feud, to substitute the White for the Red rose.
Simnel's attempt proved abortive, and Bodrugan was
compelled to seek refuge in his native Cornwall. A
writ was issued to Edgcombe for Bodrugan's arrest.
Sir Richard found him at Bodrugan. After an unsuccessful skirmish at the "woeful moor" he escaped
capture by leaping over the cliff into the sea, at a place
in Goran parish, which still bears the name of Bodrugan's Leap. On this occasion the king was able to
convince his subjects that Warwick was alive by producing him publicly and allowing him to converse
with those who knew him.

The next political adventure in which Cornwall
played a part was engineered more skilfully. There
was no available evidence that the two princes had
been murdered. It was the universal belief that Edward V had been got rid of. It was upon the assump-
tion that his brother Richard had been allowed to
escape to Flanders, that Perkin Warbeck was introduced to the world as Richard, Duke of York, or

Richard the Fourth. The story is so amazing as to be almost incredible. In the year 1491 there appeared in the streets of Cork a young man, elegantly attired—in fact, the walking advertisement of a silk merchant—one whose bearing and manner sufficed to give colour to the Yorkist assertion that he was none other than Prince Richard of York. The King of France invited him to Paris and received him as a royal prince. Margaret, Duchess of Burgundy, sister of Edward IV, acknowledged him as her nephew. In 1495 he arrived in Scotland, was received by James IV and was treated with the honour befitting the rank of the son and heir of King Edward. An allowance of £1200 a year was given him, and for a wife he was permitted to marry the Lady Catherine Gordon, daughter of the Earl of Huntly, a near relative of the Scottish king, a lady whose beauty was only equalled by her virtue and personal charm. There can be no doubt that James believed in him. The King of France invited him to Paris and assigned to him a guard of honour. In consequence, however, of the stipulations of the Treaty of Etaples, he was required to leave that country. He attended the funeral of Frederick III at Vienna as heir to the throne of England, and in 1494 accompanied in that rôle the Emperor Maximilian to Flanders. English Yorkists flocked to Flanders and offered him their swords. With these and a considerable force consisting of the adventurous jetsam of many countries, he appeared off Deal in July 1495. Henry VII, who had taken care to be informed of this, as of all other movements which threatened the peace of his kingdom, was in readiness, so that, when Perkin's exploring party came ashore, the Sheriff of Kent was enabled by craft and by ambush to seize all who escaped the deadly arrows and sword-thrusts of the Kentish men. Perkin retired to Ireland, then, as always, in a disturbed condition. He had no difficulty in securing the support of the Earl of Desmond, but his attempt to capture Waterford proved unsuccessful owing to the energy and resource of Sir Edward Poynings, the Irish Secretary. He turned once more to Scotland, which provided not only hospitality, but also tournaments in his honour. The failure, however, of the Scots to capture Berwick led to negotiations with Henry, and Perkin deemed it expedient to return to Ireland, hastened thither in all probability by news of Flamank's rebellion in Cornwall. This insurrection was owing to a tax which the people refused to pay on the ground that it was unjust that they should be called upon to pay for "a little stir of the Scots soon blown over". In this regard it is interesting to compare their action with that of Hampden's supporters in respect of ship-money, and to reflect that it was a compatriot —Attorney-General William Noy—who advised its levy throughout the country.

Flamank's rout at Blackheath took place on June 17th, 1497. Towards the end of August in that year, Perkin set sail from Cork to Cornwall. His convoy consisted of two Biscayan vessels and a Breton pinnace. On September 12th, the king wrote to Sir Gilbert Talbot

He (Perkin) has come to land in our County of Cornwall with two small ships and a Breton pinnace. Whereupon we have sent our right trusty counsellor, the Lord Daubeny our Chamberlain by land towards those parts to summon our subjects for the subduing of him and our right trusty counsellor the Lord Broke steward of our household by water with our army on the sea, now lately returned, to take the said Perkin if he return again to the sea. And we shall in our own person, if the case so require, go so accompanied thitherward, with our Lord's mercy, without delay, as we shall subdue the said Perkin and all other that will take his part if any such be. And therefore we heartily pray you to address you unto us with six score tall men on horseback defensibly arrayed and no more, without delay.[1]

Five days later Sir Henry Wentworth wrote to Sir William Calverley that he had learnt from letters addressed by the king to Lord Derby, Lord Strange and others, of Perkin's landing "in the West parts of Cornwall" and that Calverley is to be ready, when required, to serve the king with a detachment of his own men.[2]

Perkin had, in fact, landed at Whitsand Bay[3] in Sennen parish on Thursday, September 7th, and on the following Friday at Penzance, with banners displayed he had raised and moved war against the king.[4] At his landing he was accompanied by a small force of 120 men.[5] He entered the Mount without opposition, the garrison at that time being ap-

1 Ellis's *Original Letters.*   2 *Ibid.*
3 Stow, *Annals*, p. 480, ed. 1631.
4 *Baga de Secretis*, p. 217.   5 Stow, *Annals*, p. 480.

parently totally inadequate for its defence. At the
Mount he left the Lady Catherine his wife, and it
would be interesting to know what provision he made
for her comfort and security. Under ordinary circumstances there would be a complement of three
clerics, a supervisor, janitor, receiver, or his deputy, a
superintendent of works and a few families who lived
at the foot of the Mount. Perkin directed his course
towards Bodmin, his force being daily augmented by
the adhesion of discontented rebels. At Bodmin he
issued a proclamation in the name of Richard IV,[1]
and before he left that town his army amounted to
some 6000 men, one-half of whom are described as
well found. At Castle Kynok, east of the town, he
encountered Sir Peter Edgcombe, Sheriff of the
county, with a much larger force under his command,
but the latter, probably owing to their sympathy with
the rebels, refused to fight and returned home. Bon-
fires were lighted, trumpets sounded, the people acclaimed, and thus encouraged, Perkin "assumed
majesty with such a boon grace and affable de-
portment that immediately he won the affection
and admiration of all that made addresses unto
him"[2].

His stay at Bodmin must have been very brief, for
on September 17th, that is, less than a fortnight after
his landing, he was assaulting the gates of Exeter.
The assault was costly and unsuccessful, 400 of his
men being left dead on the field. Leaving Exeter he
led his men as far as Taunton where, on the 21st he

[1] Stow, *op. cit.*   [2] *Ibid.*

deserted them in the night, and betook himself to the sanctuary of the great abbey of Beaulieu. His whereabouts being discovered, he thought it best to throw himself on the king's mercy, in the hope of receiving pardon. When brought before Henry at Taunton he made a full confession of his life-history and as prisoner was brought by the king to Westminster, where he was required to repeat his confession. Thence he was led through the city to the Tower, where he remained until towards the end of 1499, when, after an attempt to escape he was seized, put on his trial and sentenced to be hanged, drawn and quartered.

Of the Lady Catherine nothing but praise has been expressed. She was left at the Mount when Perkin set forth towards Bodmin. After the debacle at Taunton, messengers were sent to apprehend and bring her to the king. Polydore Vergil gives a graphic account of Perkin's flight and the Lady Catherine's beauty.

"The King's cavalry", he says, "pushed on at speed without opposition to St Michael's Mount. There they found Perkin's wife, Catherine, and brought her a prisoner to the King. Henry marvelling at her charms regarded her as a booty, fit not for a common soldier, but for a Commander-in-Chief, and forthwith sent her to London to the Queen, with an honourable escort of matrons as the indisputable herald of the victory he had gained."[1]

[1] Equites regii interea nullis prohibentibus usque ad montem Divi Michaelis currendo pervenerunt ubi inventam Catharinam Petri uxorem, ad regem captivam duxerunt, Henricus mulieris venustatem

Whatever may have been Catherine's opinion concerning Perkin's claim it is impossible to say. She remained faithful to him, until the day of his death. Afterwards she married successively Sir Matthew Cradock, James Strangwis and Christopher Ashton, the last two having their country seats at Fyfield in Berkshire. Some confusion has arisen owing to the fact that Sir Matthew Cradock's daughter Margaret married Sir Richard Herbert and became the mother of the first Earl of Pembroke. Margaret was Sir Matthew's daughter by a former wife—Alice, daughter of Philip Mansel.

Lady Catherine does not appear to have left issue. In her will[1] there is no reference to Perkin. In it she refers to Christopher Ashton, who survived her, to her late husband James Strangwis and to "my dere and well beloved husband Sir Matthew Cradock of Cardiff". No mention is made of children and probably she left none. She died in the year 1537.[2]

After the lapse of two centuries—in 1674—two bodies were found at the foot of an old stair in the Tower and identified as those of the two princes, Edward and Richard. By order of King Charles II they were removed to King Henry's chapel in Westminster Abbey.

miratus, non militi praedam sed imperatori dignam putavit atque eam cum honesta matronarum comitatu Londinum ad reginam misit ut certam victoriae nuntiam.

[1] Her will possesses little interest apart from what has been said here. The reference is P.C.C. 10 Dyngeley.

[2] Cf. J. M. Traherne, *Hist. Notes of Sir M. Cradock*, and *Genealogist*, VI, 19.

It is possible that an echo of Warbeck's rebellion may be recognised in the fragmentary Cornish Manuscript entitled *The Duchess of Cornwall's Progress*. Mr Hamilton Jenkin has shown that a portion at least, if not all, of this manuscript was written in the Cornish language not later than the middle of the seventeenth century. *Inter alia* there is found the following:

> "Rag gun Arlothas da
> Ny en gweel gun moyha".
>
> (For our most excellent Dutchesse Right
> Unto the utmost we will fight.)

The *Progress* is the supposed record of the Duchess of Cornwall's progress to see the Land's End and to visit St Michael's Mount.[1]

There is little doubt that long before Perkin's plans were fully developed, King Henry had become cognisant of his antecedents and intentions, and there is no sufficient reason to question the general accuracy of Perkin's confession. It is, nevertheless, only fair to observe that there are living historians who regard the confession as having been manufactured for the occasion and extorted from the prisoner as the price of his exemption from the death penalty.[2]

The ringleaders only, of those who followed Perkin to Taunton, suffered the penalty of death, but heavy

---

[1] See Mr Hamilton Jenkin's valuable paper in *Roy. Inst. Cornwall*, XXI, 401–13. Also compare Botterell's *Traditions of West Cornwall*, pp. 67–72.

[2] See Mr E. Cussans, *Trans. of the Roy. Hist. Soc.*, I, 73.

fines were inflicted which reduced those, who had
lived in good condition, to beggary.

In September 1498 the king issued letters patent
to Thomas Harrys, king's chaplain, William Hatcliff
and Roger Holland to call before them

all persons of the counties of Devon and Cornwall who had
adhered to Michael Joseph (Flamank's coadjutor) rebel and
traitor, or to a certain idol or image (*idolo sive simulacro*) by
name Peter Warbeck, a man of the lowest estate, or who
aided them and who have not appeared before the King or
others, his commissaries in those parts, and submitted to the
King's grace and pardon and made fines in proportion to their
offences, and others who fled and hid themselves and still persist in their malice.

The commissaries are to impose upon them fines and
ransoms in proportion to the extent of their offences
and exact from them recognisances, securities and
bonds as well for payment of such bonds as for their
future good behaviour.[1]

The return made by the three commissaries with
the amount of the fines imposed upon those who were
supposed to have lent their support to Warbeck shows
that practically the whole county of Cornwall was
held to be liable and that in order to secure payment
manucaptors or sureties were required to be held
responsible. The manucaptors were no doubt chosen
as being men of substance and for their presumed
complicity in Perkin's escapade, otherwise the in-
justice of treating friends and enemies alike would

[1] Pat. Rolls, 14 Henry VII.

have been inexcusable and cruel. The document[1] recording the names of the delinquents with the amount of their fines which is given in the Appendix, has not hitherto been printed and is valuable to the historian and genealogist alike.

[1] P.R.O. E 101, 516, 27; Appendix, p. 191

Governors and Receivers of the Mount

THE name of Peter St Aubyn, described as of Helston and St Michael's Mount appears among those of the manucaptors. He was held liable for the payment of the fines inflicted upon the parishes of Helston, Sithney and Crowan, for his complicity or supposed complicity in Warbeck's rebellion. Whatever course he may have taken amid the turmoil of that unfortunate affair appears to have been satisfactorily explained, for in the year 1508 he succeeded Sir Richard Nanfan as receiver and governor of St Michael's Mount and had in the same year, together with Peter Bevill of Gwarnick, esquire, John Godolphin, esquire, Thomas Tregoos of Penpoll, gentleman, and John Bevill of Marketjew, gentleman—merchant tinners—the king's pardon for having broken the Stannary laws.[1] In 1511 Peter St Aubyn was appointed a commissioner of array. His Compotus Roll for the year 1514, giving an account of the farm of the Mount, is preserved at Hatfield.

At this point it will be useful to consider the status of the receiver of an alien priory. Ordinarily he was a steward who administered a priory's possessions, and sent in a yearly return of its receipts and expenditure commonly called a compotus. So long as the priory of St Michael's Mount was regarded as a cell of the abbey of Mont St Michel, its steward no doubt

[1] State Papers, 1508.

sent an apport of sixteen marks to the abbot in fulfil-
ment of the terms of the charter of 1135, and paid
over to the prior, after deducting salaries and expenses,
the remainder of the profits. Its domestic affairs were
no concern of the civil authority. When Normandy
was lost to the English crown in the reign of King
John, the relation of the priory to the parent house
theoretically remained the same, but the administra-
tion of its revenue, a portion of which was payable to
a foreign lord, naturally involved a closer scrutiny on
the part of the English king's officers. The priory became appendant to the earldom[1] and subsequently to
the Duchy of Cornwall.[2] The question of the priory's
relationship to the abbey appears to have remained
uncertain. In 1337, by an ordinance in council, a
general seizure of alien priories
took place. The priory of St
Michael's Mount was visited by
William Herdeshall, chaplain,
and John Hamely, Sheriff of
Cornwall, and a careful survey
made of its possessions. This
ordinance also required that certain persons in each county
should be appointed to have
charge of the temporalities and
to pay the monks a fixed stipend.
For this purpose Sir Ralph
Bloyou, Lord of the Manor of Truthwall in Ludgvan

BLOYOU

Argent a saltira engrailed
sable

---

[1] Inq. p.m. Edmund, Earl of Cornwall, 1301.
[2] *Ibid.* Edward, Duke of Cornwall, 1379.

parish, was appointed receiver at the Mount. This, however, appears to have been only a temporary expedient adopted on account of the war with France. The appointment of prior was, moreover, subject to the king's approval, for in 1395 the Abbot of Mont St Michel petitioned the king—to allow him to appoint. The king consented on condition that the appointee was an adherent of Pope Boniface IX and of good behaviour to the king and his people.[1] Whether the abbot exercised the power so granted it is impossible to say. Richard Auncell became prior in 1385 and was *restored* by letters patent to the priory in 1399. He is therein described as a monk of the (Benedictine) abbey of Tavistock and, as Prior of St Michael's Mount, he is required to render yearly to the king during the war with France the ancient apport due, in time of peace, to the chief house of the priory beyond the seas and to support the monks and others and to pay to the king the tenths, fifteenths and other subsidies granted by the clergy and commonalty of the realm.[2]

Prior Auncell's troubles were not at an end. Three years later an Act of Parliament was passed confiscating to the crown all priories which were not conventual, and under this act the priory of St Michael's Mount was illegally seized. The good ship St Michael found it difficult to avoid shipwreck between the Scylla of convent and the Charybdis of cell. As convent the king had claimed to appoint her prior, as

[1] Pat. Rolls, 1391–6, p. 625.
[2] *Ibid.* 1399, p. 70.

cell she was seized by the Act of 1402, and Auncell must pay £20 yearly for it. The matter was settled satisfactorily in the following year when a fresh grant of the priory was made to Auncell on condition that he rendered to the king £10 yearly during the war with France,[1] that is, one mark less than the ancient apport payable to the parent house. This decision appears to have been accepted as final. The priory was conventual, severed from the abbey of Mont St Michel and the apport, if any, accrued to the crown. It remained for Henry V to foreshadow its future as a religious house. As such it is dealt with elsewhere. Here it will suffice to say that the priory with its possessions were given, in accordance with Henry's directions, to the Bridgettine convent at Isleworth, and its receiver was expected to send a yearly return of its revenue to the Exchequer although it was entirely devoted towards the convent's support.

In 1345 the priory had been in farm by the prior himself.[2] It was so in 1432 when William Morton, described as Archpriest of the Mount, furnished a return which showed that there was owing to Robert Hay the sum of £19. 13s. 10d., John Godolphin £63. 6s. 8d. and to himself £44. 11s. 6d. This debt amounting to little short of £3000 of our money had doubtless been incurred in the construction of a stone quay for the better protection of ships seeking shelter in Mount's Bay. Usually the receiver of the Mount was a person of high rank in the county who

[1] Pat. Rolls, 6, Dec. 1403.
[2] Oliver's *Monasticon*, p. 425.

employed a deputy to perform his duties. He was styled variously, sometimes as farmer, sometimes as receiver, sometimes as receiver-general. Both before and after Warbeck's rebellion we find him otherwise distinguished as sheriff, ex-sheriff and commissioner of array. In 1482 it was John Fortescue, esquire, in 1488 Sir Richard Edgcombe, in 1490 Sir Richard Nanfan and in 1513 Peter St Aubyn,[1] esquire, who filled the office of receiver for the Abbess of Syon. On this account we may perhaps conclude that the appointee was one who was required to be equally acceptable to the crown and the abbess.

For some years before Peter St Aubyn became Governor of the Mount the family of Bevill had been in some way interested in its welfare. In the year 1490 Peter Bevill, Peter Tregos and Thomas St Aubyn were appointed commissioners to array fencible men of Cornwall and to place beacons for warning the people of the king's enemies.[2] Peter Bevill died in 1511, and in his will bequeathed a sum of money for the beacon light of St Michael's Mount (*lumini Sti Michis in Monte*)—a light which three-quarters of a century later signalled the approach of the Armada and inspired Macaulay,

For swift to east and swift to west the ghastly war flame spread,
High on St Michael's Mount it shone; it shone on Beachy Head.

---

[1] *Cartulary.*
[2] State Papers, Henry VII, p. 322.

John, the son of Peter Bevill, described as of St Michael's Mount, died before his father. In his will he directs that his body shall be buried in the church of the Mount.[1]

In 1511 war was declared against France, and two years afterwards the battle of Spurs was fought and won by Henry VIII. In the meanwhile the enemy's navy was by no means inactive and ventured to invade the coast of Sussex. The English fleet under Sir Edward Howard, which included two ships of the first class, the *Regent* and the *Sovereign* sent from Plymouth, fought a desperate engagement in which the English were successful, but with the loss of the *Regent* which blew up and sank, carrying with her her two commanders Sir John Carew and Sir Thomas Knevit.

Richard Carew the historian, who lived at a time sufficiently approximate to the event, tells us that "Marketjew now felt the Frenchmen's fiery indignation". They entered Mount's Bay and effected a landing a little east of Marazion, plundered and afterwards set fire to the town, which was completely burnt to the ground. But, says Carew, "the smoke of those poor houses alarming the country made the place over hot for the enemy's any longer abode". Their flight was no doubt owing to the array of "the fencibles", a force which had been brought into being by Henry VII in 1490 as already stated. Hals, who

---

[1] By his will, dated April 18th, 1433, Sir John Arundell leaves to the light in St Michael's Mount 13*s*. 4*d*. and *operi cancellae ibidem faciendae* 13*s*. 4*d*.

is quoted by Polwhele (in a footnote) and others, attributes the retreat of the enemy to the activity of John Carminow the sheriff, but no reliance can be placed upon his assertion which is unsupported by evidence.[1]

St Michael's Mount was evidently the enemy's objective, but its garrison and castle were too strong to invite attack and the garrison too few in number to protect the town.

As the result, however, of this raid steps were immediately taken to provide strong defences for the outposts on Mount's Bay. Two maps of this date may be seen in the British Museum which were evidently made for this purpose.[2] One of them, coloured, illustrates the Mount and its relation to the surrounding coast from Cuddan Point to Mousehole with measurements of the distances of those places and of Penlee Point and Penzance from the Mount, on the land side of which in harbour are three ocean-going vessels. The other map shows "fortifications not made" at Penlee and Penzance and also "the Egges where the Frenchmen londyd" which appears as a small creek east and very near Marras Jowe (Market-jew).

Peter St Aubyn, Governor of the Mount, was the second son of Thomas St Aubyn of Clowance by his wife Mary Trenouth and brother of Thomas St

---

[1] Lest the reader should suspect the writer of prejudice it may be allowable to direct his attention to Hals' statement respecting the manor of Lanistley and the transparent forgery of a charter in its support.   [2] Cott. Aug. I. I. 34.

Aubyn who married Mary, daughter of Sir Thomas Grenville of Stowe. Letters of Thomas St Aubyn, dated 1530, addressed to his wife's sister Honor, Viscountess Lisle, have been preserved.[1] Honor Grenville's first husband was Sir John Basset of Umberleigh, lord of Tehidy, and Thomas St Aubyn was probably executor or trustee during the heir's minority, who was at that time nine years of age. In one of his letters he informs Lady Lisle that the tin mine at Carn Kye (near Redruth parish church) is proving satisfactory, and thanks her for the coneys of Tehidy, his own at Clowance having become scarce. In another he styles himself "your own Kanaffe" and sends a dozen puffins. In another, referring to Tehidy, he tells her that "as for the hedge that Harry Nanse made, it is now abroad like feathers of a goose new pollyd (polled) by a hungry fox".

Peter St Aubyn, whose Compotus Roll for 1513 is preserved at Hatfield, was succeeded in the office of receiver by Humphry Arundell, who had married the widow of Peter Bevill, son of the Peter Bevill of whom mention has been made.

The last grant made by the Abbess of Syon of the farm of the Mount is of exceptional interest, and cannot be better described than in the words of a Patent Roll of the second year of Queen Elizabeth[2] which reads as follows:

Whereas Agnes, Abbess of the monastery of St Saviour and the Blessed Virgin Mary and St Bridget of Syon in Middlesex

---

[1] Gairdner's *Letters and Papers*, VI.
[2] Pat. Rolls, 2 Eliz., Part 4, m. 42.

of the Order of St Augustine, and her convent by an indenture dated 4th of February 25 Henry VIII (1533) demised to John Melyton of Pengarseke in Cornwall and William Melyton his son their farm of St Michael's Mount with all lands, tenements, rents, tithes and profits belonging to the same which John Melyton formerly held by pretext of a demise to him by the said Abbess and Convent dated 8th of November 13 Henry VIII (1521) with reversion to the Abbess and Convent and her successors of all oblations, gifts, advowsons and benefits and the same Abbess and Convent also granted to the said John Melyton and William his son the command and custody of the said Mount to hold the said captaincy and all the said premises for thirty years at an annual rent at Easter and Michaelmas of £26. 13s. 4d.

And the said John and William agreed during that term to find two priests and one clerk, under the archpriest to reside within the said Mount to celebrate daily there, and a janitor.

Now after the death of John Melyton, William Melyton has the whole right and title in the premises and has surrendered the same to be cancelled. The Queen now grants to William Melyton the whole farm of St Michael at the Mount and the whole site, house, mansions or corporeal messuage called St Michael's Mount formerly belonging to the monastery of Syon in Middlesex to hold for forty years at an annual rent of £26. 13s. 4d.

This lease granted in 1560 was for a term of forty years. In it no provision was made for the defence of the Mount or for religious worship. The priory had ceased to exist early in the fifteenth century and the archpresbytery which had taken its place in or about 1539. Leland who wrote on the eve of its confiscation tells us that "the captaynes and prestes lodgings were in the south syde and west of S. Mich. chapel".

William Milliton died before the expiration of his lease, and in 1596 a lease was granted by the crown to Arthur Harris. This required him to repair and maintain the pier and to find five soldiers for the defence of the Mount and to render to the crown a yearly rent of £26. 13s. 4d.

Arthur Harris came of a West Country family of distinction, which for five generations at least had preserved an unbroken descent in the male line. The original seat of the family was Radford. By the marriage of William Harris with Thomasine, co-heiress of Walter Hayne, the Hayne estate in Devon passed to his grandson and namesake. Arthur Harris, Captain of the Mount, was son and heir of the latter. In 1602 he acquired the mansion and demesne lands of Kenegie by purchase from John Tripcony, grandson of John Tripcony, who had obtained it in like manner from the Stowells.

Few houses in West Cornwall are more worthy of preservation. It is delightfully situated. Near the main entrance from the high road is a "gazebo" or look-out which commands a unique view of Mount's Bay, and the inscriptions on the slate sedilia of it are quaint and interesting. Here the Harris family lived for several generations. The following pedigree, which differs in some respects from that given by Burke and Vivian, illustrates the devolution of the estate.

William Harris = (1) Mary Greville
             (2) Honor d. of Sir William
                   Godolphin and widow of
                   William Milliton

Arthur Harris = Margaret Daville
Captain of the Mount
Bought Kenegie 1602

John Harris of Hayne   William Harris = Philippa Noy,
                       m. 1627   niece of the
Sir Arthur Harris Bt.   d. 1661   Atty General

Christopher Harris = Elizabeth   William   John
b. 1633 d. 1722   Martin   b. 1638   b. 1642
                                      o.s.p.

William Harris = Jane St Aubyn   Lydia ux.
b. 1653 m. 1685   John Borlase
Oct. 7

Christopher Harris William Harris John H.   Jane ux.
o.s.p. 1775   s.p.   William Arundel

Christopher Harris = Penelope Donnithorne

Elizabeth ux. Isaac Donnithorne
who assumed the name of Harris

It is remarkable, though quite consistent with Cornish tradition, that among those who took part in the attempt to place James, Duke of Monmouth, on the throne there should be found a number of Cornishmen. Among these were "Christopher Harris, esquire, and William Harris, gentleman, and Hugh Ladner, all of Gulval".

The foregoing pedigree shows that Christopher Harris had a brother William and a son William. The William whose name occurs in the indictment was probably Christopher's brother. The battle of Sedgemoor which decided the fate of that unhappy enterprise was fought on July 6th, 1688, and was followed by the inhuman brutality of Kirke's *Lambs* and the Bloody Assize of Judge Jeffreys. How Christopher Harris and his brother William became entangled in the mad scheme and how they managed to escape its consequences is not known. Judge Jeffreys did not scruple to accept bribes, and it is possible that he did so in dealing with the Harrises. Exactly three months after the battle of Sedgemoor William, the son of Christopher Harris, married Jane, the daughter of John St Aubyn, esquire, of Clowance. The above pedigree gives their descendants at Kenegie.

HARRIS OF
HAYNE

Sable three crescents in
a border argent

To resume our story, among the Salisbury Manuscripts, as edited by the Historical Manuscripts Commission,[1] there are three documents which throw

[1] XIII, 393.

light upon the events of the latter half of the sixteenth century. The first is a letter dated July 22nd, 1586, in which John Fitz and John Hale inform Lord Burleigh that at three o'clock in the afternoon one Mr Richard Hawkins, a gentleman of Sir Francis Drake, came from the Mount where he landed, being driven from his general by tempest, and wishes to apprise the queen of his arrival. The second letter undated is a petition from the Captain of the Mount to the Council. He states that the commissioners appointed for viewing that place have certified that the queen has only two pieces of iron ordnance there, and that eight or nine men will serve for continual guard if 200 or 150 of the inhabitants of the adjoining parishes may be always at command to serve there. He prays for the necessary ordnance and munitions and that order may be given for the guard as shall be thought convenient and for its charge to be imposed upon him: he submits himself thereunto according to the bond in which he is bound to obey the order of the Lord Treasurer, the Lord Admiral and Sir John Fortescue. He asks authority to make choice of the three next parishes to train and exercise them for the defence of the place, they being exempt from service elsewhere. A note at the foot states "that this was never delivered". It is endorsed "Petition of Sir Arthur Harris, Esq., Captain of the Mount". The third letter is a similar petition, which was delivered in which Mr Harris, Captain of St Michael's Mount, begs to be supplied with some pieces of ordnance and, in regard to the present danger, with a reasonable quantity of powder and shot for the defence of the same: and also that he may have authority to make choice of the fittest men of the three next parishes to be trained and exercised for that purpose upon extraordinary occasion. It was probably in answer to the repeated applications of Captain Arthur Harris that we find amongst the Egerton MSS. the following letter, dated June 14th, 1584. To whom it was addressed is not stated; possibly it was sent to the Sheriff of Cornwall.

Fortification of St Michael's Mount

After my harty commendations. Whereas there has been request made by the Captn. of the Castle of St Michael's Mount in Cornwall to be served with a proportion of ordnance and munitions contayned in the note herein closed, these are to pray you both to send word which of these kinds you are able to furnish out of the store and what must be provided by emption, and also find a warrant ready drawn for that of so much as I have rated in schedule. And so I bid you hartily farewell From the court at Richmond 14 June 1584.

Endorsed on the second page in another's handwriting.

Cornwall   St Michael's Mount

'One demi culverin
'One saker of iron
'200 shot for both
'Cariage and other furniture
'20 calivers furnished
'One last of canon corne
'Two berrals of caliver powther
'$\frac{1}{2}$ hundreth weight of match'.

In another's handwriting

'A quarter of a last one berral'.

It is clear that Arthur Harris was in charge of St Michael's Mount before his lease of 1596 was granted, and also that he realised fully his rights and responsibilities. In 1591 Sir Francis Godolphin and Mr Moohan (Mohun) lodged a complaint against Arthur Harris, esquire, that one Robert Johnson to whom the queen had granted a gunner's room in the castle of St Michael's Mount and a fee of eightpence a day, had been refused payment of the same.[1] The rebuke administered to the Captain of the Mount whether deserved or otherwise is a masterpiece which betrays the source of its inspiration in the haughty queen whose will was supreme and whose temper was sometimes uncertain.

The letter may be given in full. It is addressed to Sir Arthur Harris and reads as follows:

We commend us unto you. Whereas it pleased the Queen's Majesty to grant unto Robert Johnson the room of a "cannonier" within the Castle of St Michael's Mount in regard of the hurts and maims he hath received in her Highness' service, whereunto the poor man complaineth ye do oppose yourself, pretending the choice of those persons to appertain properly to you, and therefore do refuse to accomplish her direction in that behalf. These are to let you understand that her Majesty having knowledge of the undutiful respect you have had unto her grant and to the letters written

[1] *Acts of the P.C.*, eodem anno.

unto you from us signifying her absolute pleasure in the same, do not a little marvel thereat, and hath commanded us to let you know that if you shall continue your wilful refusal in this case, that her purpose is to draw your pretended rights in question, whereof it will behove you to have better consideration as you tender her Majesty's gracious favour and your own good. And to conclude, if these our letters and her Majesty's pleasure thereby signified notwithstanding, you shall persist in refusing to admit the said Johnson to the place, then are you required forthwith to make your appearance before us and yield some better reason thereof than hitherto hath been delivered whereof (wherefore) fail us not as you will answer to the contrary at your peril.

We are not informed concerning the result of this terrible threat. All we know is that Arthur Harris retained his position as Captain of the Mount. The letters to and from the Privy Council were written in the year 1591,[1] and the lease of the Mount to him was granted in 1596. From the latter date until his death he was both lessee and captain. His request contained in the third letter of 1588, namely, that a reserve force should be recruited from the fittest men in the neighbouring parishes and trained in case of emergency seems to have been granted, for in the interesting correspondence[1] of Thomas St Aubyn, Francis Godolphin, H. Nance and Nicholas Parker between the years 1592 and 1600 we find a muster order issued by Nicholas Parker, Thomas St Aubyn, Hannibal Vyvyan and Thomas Chyverton addressed

[1] *Acts of the P.C.* XXI, pp. 391, 459.
[2] B. Mus. Add. 34,224, fols. 7, 8, 15, 25, 38, 39.

to the captains of companies dated April 1600 in which they state

For that the time of the year now is like to be fair and the days long we think fit to take a view of your companies with their arms for the discharging of our duties and the readiness of the country for service and defence of the same if need shall require. Therefore these are to pray and require you to be before us with your company complete and armed at Helston Downe on Tuesday in the Whitsun week next by nine of the clock in the forenoon to be viewed mustered and trained where we will continue you and them till Wednesday two or three of the clock in the afternoon, if we see occasion. And that for every caliver there be brought half a pound of powder and for every musket three quarters of a pound with match proportionable and some bullets.

The constables of the several parishes are to assist them in furnishing a true account of the arms and ammunition kept therein.

At the end there is a memorandum or postscript in Thomas St Aubyn's handwriting in which it is stated that the original of the above of which this is a true copy has been sent to his cousin Basset. The order is franked: Clowance, April 28th, 1600.

The lease of the Mount granted to Arthur Harris was for life.[1] The deeds at Hatfield show that the fee simple of it was acquired by Robert, Earl of Salisbury, in the closing years of the reign of Queen Elizabeth. On March 19th, 1602, the Earl wrote to Thomas Rosewarren, Mayor of Marazion, as follows:

I have purchased of the Queen's Majesty the manor of

[1] State Papers, 1617.

St Michael's Mount in Cornwall whereof the town of Mark-asue is a member. I would be glad to have some particulars, knowledge of the royalties and liber-ties belonging to me, and meanwhile, the sheriffs or justices of the peace to forbear any proceedings until they receive further order thereon. To Thomas Rosewarren Mayor of Markasue.

In 1604 the keeper of the deeds of the late Court of Aug-mentations delivered to Viscount Cranborne for his scrutiny those relating to St Michael's Mount, and in 1612 the crown finally confirmed to him—he had been created Earl of Salisbury in 1605 —the Mount and its possessions. The lease to Arthur Harris still held good.

CECIL, EARL OF SALISBURY

Barry of ten argent and azure with six scutcheons sable each charged with a lion argent and the difference of a crescent

In 1617 an inventory of the ordnance was made and a survey of the reparations.[1] Ten years later in a letter to Secretary Conway Arthur Harris solicits his attention to these matters and sends his kinsman Hannibal Vyvyan to urge upon him the need of dispatch.[2] The next year (January 15th, 1628) his importunity is renewed. The danger of the times, the situation of the Mount and its small store of ammuni-tion call for immediate action. A final appeal is made in the following month in which he prays that order

[1] State Papers, Feb. 1617.   [2] *Ibid.* 1628.

may be given for supply and repair of the castle according to a survey of the commissioners made four years ago; also that the ordinary allowance of six hundredweight of powder may be increased. This, accompanied by a certificate of Richard Moryson and others of the necessary repairs is estimated at £24. Arthur Harris died on May 16th in the same year and was buried in Gulval Church, where a monument enumerates his virtues at great length.

In the following January William, Earl of Salisbury, writes to Secretary Conway: "There has lately fallen to my hands, by the decease of Arthur Harris the fort of St Michael's Mount and John Harris, heir of Arthur, scruples to deliver up the store of powder without a warrant". He prays the secretary to obtain one sufficient for his discharge.

Here it may be convenient, for the purpose of reference, to state that in 1640 William, Earl of Salisbury, sold the Mount to Sir Francis Basset of Tehidy, and that in 1659 John, son and heir of Sir Francis Basset, levied a fine conveying the same to John St Aubyn, Esq., of Clowance.

The death of Arthur Harris deprived the Mount of a very zealous officer. His successor was Hannibal Newman. A conspectus of the situation as it existed between the years 1628 and 1659 when Colonel John St Aubyn petitioned the Lord Protector that the Mount might be saved from decay and destruction is afforded by the reply and reports rendered.[1] Colonel Robert Bennet was sent to report and to examine the

[1] Deeds *penes* Lord St Levan at St Michael's Mount.

title of the Commonwealth. The following purport to be the results of his enquiry. Thomas Slade whose father was gunner in the time of Mr Arthur Harris reports that the Mount has been maintained for the Supreme Magistrate of England and a flag sent in King James's name, and that he hath been commanded in the king's name to keep watch and ward and protect the king's ships, that guns and ammunition have been supplied by the king and that the key (quay) and pier were maintained by the king's excise. Ezechiell Arundell, Hannibal Newman, John Colling, clerk, and Thomas Slade reported that

Queen Elizabeth to whom the church and patrimony had fallen gave the same to the Earl of Salisbury upon these conditions,—that the Earl out of the revenues of the Mount (should) continue a guard of soldiers and defend it. Accordingly the Earl did maintain a garrison consisting of a Captain, Governor, Gunner and eight private soldiers until he sold the same to Sir Francis Basset who had £200 allowance in the purchase to do the same. Under him there was a Chief Commander—one Captain Harris and after him Captain Hannibal Newman for 30 years, who received from the Earl £50 per annum and his gunner £12 and each of the eight soldiers £8. This was so until Francis Basset bought the Mount and the said Newman obtained his arms and ammunition from the Tower of London.

They further report that a flag has been sent in the king's name and the garrison supported by the royal bounty. The document bears the signature of Richard Lepyean who was probably clerk of the Commission.

Hannibal Newman's death is recorded in the Gulval
Register as having taken place on August 18th, 1659.

It does not fall within purview of this narrative to
discuss the course of events which led to the Great
Rebellion. It must suffice to say that it was political
and religious and, in not a few instances, involved
the severance of friendships and family ties. Many
families were saved from irreparable disaster by
reason of the very fact that some members were for
the king and some for the parliament. In Cornwall—
as will be seen from the Cornish Articles of War
drawn up in September 1642—the leaders of the
parliamentary forces, of whom Sir Richard Buller
and Alexander Carew were chief, decreed the death
penalty against those who "shall use anie trayterous
words against his majesty's sacred person or royall
Authority". In the same month of the same year a
prisoner captured by the royalists and released, describing his examination before Sir Bevile Grenville,
relates that when he told them that his leaders were
Sir Richard Buller and Alexander Carew, Sir Bevile
remarked, "Mr Carew and Sir Richard Buller are
two wise men but they make the whole country fools.
They pretend that they fight for the King but they
'would cutt his throate if they coulde and soe they
would ours too'".[1] This probably fairly represents
the respective attitudes of those who were for the
parliament and those who were for the king, in the
earlier stages of the war. The former claimed to defend the king and parliament, the latter the king. In

1 *Buller Papers*, privately printed, pp. 63 and 71.

the western half of the county we find Arundells, Bassets and Vyvyans on the side of the king, Boscawens, Trefusises and Eriseys with the parliament; and St Aubyn, Godolphins and Courtenays with both. In the beginning, in Cornwall, the king was successful. The victory gained by Sir Ralph Hopton and Sir Bevile Grenville at Stratton in the spring of 1643 was of so decisive a character that for the space of one year hostilities were suspended. The king signified his appreciation of the exploits in the letter of thanks which is frequently to be found in Cornish churches. Sir Francis Basset

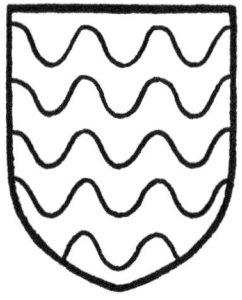

BASSET OF
TEHIDY
Barry wavy or and
gules

who had become possessed of the Mount in 1640 and who was, in 1643, sheriff of the county and probably present at the battle, writing twelve days later from Truro to his wife, thus expresses his joy.

Dearest Soule

Oh deare soule, prayse God everlastingly. Reade the enclosed, ringe out the bells, rayse bonfyres, publish these joyfull tydings. Believe these truths, excuse my writing larger, I have no tyme; wee march on to meete of victorious friends, and to seaze all the rebells left if wee can finde such livinge. Your dutyous prayers God has heard. Bless us accordingly, pray everlastingly, and Jane and Betty and all you owne. Thy owne, Fras. Basset. Pray let my cousin Harry know these joyfull blessings. Send word to the ports south and north, to searche narrowly for all strangers travelling for passage and cause the keepinge them close and safe.

To my dearest dearest friend Mrs Basset at the Mount

Speed this, haste, haste.

In the latter half of the year 1644 hostilities were renewed. The king and Prince Maurice entered Cornwall with Lord Goring as commander-in-chief and the Earl of Essex assumed command of the parliamentary forces. The queen, who was at Pendennis Castle, departed for France. Sir Francis Basset in a letter to his wife at the Mount describes her as "the most worne and weake pitifull creature in the world" doubtless the result of care and anxiety. The autumn campaign proved favourable to the royalists. Sir Francis Basset appears to have been the director of munitions, with a depot at the Mount. He writes from Lostwithiel to

"Mrs Basset, my dear wife at her Tehidy"...."Here is infinite want of match.[1] For God's sake send to Mr Lane as soon as this comes to yr. hands and cause him with all speede to press horses and bring away six hundred weight of match from the Mount to this army first to Lostwithiel and thence to this army....Pray let Jacke write to me truely what match he has in all, and I conjure you both to get as much as possible to be made with all possible haste at what coste soever."

As a postscript he adds "I thank Christ I am very gracious with King and Prince".

By the end of 1644 Cornwall was entirely in the

[1] Gunpowder (?).

king's hands. On September 5th he left the county. Sir Francis Basset to Lady Basset—"his perfect Joy"—on the eve of the king's departure tells her that "the King in leaving, in the hearing of thousands, as soon as he saw him cried Dear Mr Sheriff I leave Cornwall to you safe and sound". Alas! it was not for long. Sir Francis died a fortnight later, and the Mount and its garrison passed to his brother, Sir Arthur Basset, who in the following November removed the Duke of Hamilton from Pendennis to the Mount.

On August 25th of this year Lord Hopton, then at Liskeard, in a report to Sir Francis states,

I have seen St Michael's Mount and conceive it to be a place of great importance to be kept out of the enemy's hands both in respect of the strength of the place, as also of the consequence of the Mount's Pier for safety of the ships whereby use may be made of them; in all cases I think it therefore very requisite his Majesty should be moved to make convenient allowance of fifty or sixty men to be in garrison there during the war and allowance for them of £500 or £600 a year out of delinquents' estates and the command of it to Sir Francis Basset whose heritage it is.

As the result of this report the king granted[1] the governorship of the Mount to Sir Francis Basset, who was thereby authorised to call in one hundred voluntary soldiers for the defence of the same. He is to have £500 out of the estates of John Silly,[2] gent., and Richard and John, both his sons.

[1] Charter at St Michael's Mount.   [2] (?) Ceely.

Nothing of importance transpired during 1645. The Prince of Wales left Cornwall for Scilly in the spring of the following year, which was one of disaster to the royalists. Sir Richard Grenville, Sir Bevile's brother, who had already incurred Lord Goring's displeasure by reason of his tyrannical conduct, on the arrival of Goring's successor, Lord Hopton, as commander-in-chief, refused to obey orders and was committed to Launceston prison and afterwards to the Mount. Lord Hopton was defeated by Sir Thomas Fairfax at Torrington and pursued by him into Cornwall. Deserted by some of the principal persons in the county, threatened with mutiny of his officers, he was compelled to allow his army to capitulate at Truro, and repaired to the Mount whence he embarked in order to join the prince in Scilly. On April 23rd, 1646, St Michael's Mount surrendered owing, it is said, to the advice tendered by the Duke of Hamilton. Sir Arthur Basset, by the terms of the surrender was allowed to depart with his retinue to Scilly. The capture embraced 30 pieces of ordnance, 3 murdering pieces, 80 tuns of wine, 100 barrels of gunpowder, 500 muskets and 100 pikes.[1]

On June 17th, 1647, the Lords and Commons nominated Colonel John St Aubyn to be Captain of the Mount. Colonel St Aubyn had filled the office of sheriff in 1643; he represented St Ives in parliament in 1659 and 1660 and Michell in 1679. In 1659 he was appointed vice-admiral and in that year

[1] State Papers, 1646.

took up his residence at the Mount. His appeal to the Lord Protector in the same year that the Mount might be saved from decay and the reports of the consequent enquiry have been already described. Among the St Aubyn muniments is preserved General Monk's order to Colonel Robert Bennett to hand over his command to Colonel St Aubyn. It is a model of clearness, directness and brevity and reads as follows:

You are on sight hereof to disband those men under your command in the garrison of St Michael's Mount in the County of Cornwall and to deliver up the possession of the house unto Colonel John St Aubyn with all the ordnance arms ammunition and provisions of war and victual therein to be by him kept and possessed for the use of the state and you are to take a receipt under the hand of the said Col. St Aubyn of what particulars you shall so have or deliver and send me a double of them. Given under my hand 12 March 1659. George Monck. To Col. Robert Bennett.

It will be observed that the letter is dated the day before that on which parliament effaced from its journals the pledge of fidelity to the republic as then constituted (without king or House of Lords). Monk was supreme and, in order to maintain his supremacy until the time came for him to surrender the reins of government into the king's hands, he immediately cashiered all the officers of his army of whose fidelity he entertained suspicion. This probably did not apply to Colonel Bennett. As we have seen he had been sent to report upon the Mount's dilapidations and requirements. Since its surrender to the parliament it had been the headquarters of the parliamentary army, one of whose most zealous officers was Major Peter Ceely. In the grant of the governorship by King Charles to Sir Francis Basset we saw that for its defence Sir Francis was to receive £500 out of the estates of John Silly, gent., and Richard and John his two sons. The Ceelys (or Sillys) were merchants at Plymouth and at St Ives. Of the latter borough Peter Ceely was mayor in 1650 and one of its representatives in parliament in 1659. In 1655 he had a captain's commission from the Protector, and in a letter dated January 4th, 1659, he writes to Captain Francis Arundell (of Trengwainton) and orders him to proceed with his squadron to Penzance in case of tumult and adds, "if you see occasion you may quarter your squadron at St Just keeping intelligence with the Mount". Colonel St Aubyn, who took up his abode at the Mount, was the last of the governors to maintain a garrison therein. Judging from the numerous and responsible offices he was called upon to fill as a soldier, admiral, member of parliament, sheriff and governor, and from the impress he has left on the interior of the castle, he must have been a great gentleman and sportsman. His son Sir John St Aubyn, the first baronet, decided to live at Clowance which had been the seat of the St Aubyn family from the fourteenth century, and it was not until the middle of the nineteenth century that Sir Edward St Aubyn, baronet, grandfather of the present owner, Brigadier-General Lord St Levan, made the Mount his permanent abode. During the interval, however, the fabric of the castle and church was not neglected. The Mount appears to have been maintained throughout that time as an occasional or additional residence and, as such, to have received constant attention.

Alterations were made in 1720. The church was repaired in 1811 and the beautiful glass of the rose windows inserted. In 1727 and 1728 Sir John St Aubyn, the third baronet, practically rebuilt the pier, which was enlarged in 1824.

Under the direction of the late Mr J. P. St Aubyn the entire range of buildings was overhauled and additions made to meet modern conditions.

It would be difficult to find an ancient building which has suffered less from the indiscretion, ignorance and vandalism of the so-called restorer than St Michael's Mount.

ST AUBYN, LORD ST LEVAN

Ermine a cross gules with five bezants thereon

Dr Johnson once composed an inscription for a house in the Midlands. It is perhaps faulty in some respects, but it expresses a hope which will be shared by everyone in a twofold sense who knows the Mount and its noble owner.

Stet domus haec donec testudo perambulet orbem
Ebibat et donec fluctus formica marinos.

Appendix

I

LEOFRIC'S GRANT OF FREEDOM FROM EPISCOPAL CONTROL

Ego quidem Levricus Deo dono Essecestriae episcopus jussione et exhortatione domini mei reverentissimi Gregorii papae regisque nostri et reginae omniumque optimatum totius regni Angliae exhortatus ut ecclesiam Beati Michaelis archangeli de Cornubia, utpote quae officio et ministerio angelico creditur atque comprobatur consecrari et sanctificari, quatenus eam ob omni episcopali jure potestate, seu subjectione liberarem atque exuerem, quod et facere totius cleri nostri consensu et hortatu non distuli, libero igitur eam et exuo ab omni episcopali dominatione, subjectione et inquietudine, et omnibus illis qui illam ecclesiam suis cum beneficiis et elemosinis expetierint et visitaverint, tertiam partem penitentiarum condonamus. Et ut hoc inconcussum et immobile et etiam inviolabile fine tenus permaneat, ex authoritate Patris et Filii et Spiritus sancti omnibus nostris successoribus interdicimus ne aliquid contra hoc decretum usurpare praesumant.

II

WILLIAM OF WORCESTER'S VERSION[1]

Universis sanctae matris ecclesiae presentes litteras inspecturis vel audituris salutem: noverit universitas vestra quod sanctissimus dominus papa Gregorius, anno ab incarnatione domini,

[1] Supplementary Papers, *Parl. Hist. of Cornwall*, p. 96.

millessimo septuagesimo, ad ecclesiam montis Sancti Michaelis in tumba in comitatu Cornubiae gerens eximiae devocionis affectum, pie concessit ecclesiae predictae quae ministerio angelico creditur et comprobatur consecrari et sanctificari, (et) omnibus fidelibus qui illam ecclesiam cum suis beneficiis et elemosinis expecierint seu visitaverint tertiam partem penitenciarum suarum eis condonari. Et ut inconcussum et inviolabile fine tenus permaneat ex autoritate Dei patris omnipotentis et Filii et Spiritus Sancti omnibus successoribus suis interdixit, ne quid contra hoc decretum usurpare presumant. Ista verba in antiquis regestris de novo in hac ecclesia repertis inventa, prout hic in valvis ecclesiae publice ponuntur. Et quia pluribus istud est incognitum, ideo nos in Christo Dei famuli et ministri hujus ecclesiae universitatem vestram, qui regimen animarum possidetis, ob mutuae vicissitudinis obtentum requirimus et rogamus, quatinus ista publicetis in ecclesiis vestris ut vestri subditi et subjecti ad majorem exortacionem devotionis attencius animentur, et locum istum gloriosius peregrinando frequentent ad dona (prebenda) et indulgencias predicta(s) graciose consequenda(s).

III

IN LAUDEM MICHAELIS ET ANGELORUM OMNIUM IN TEMPLO MICHAELIS SACRO[1]

1. Porro tu primas tibi vindicato
   Carminis palles Michael beate
   Primipilati duce quo triumphant
   Agmina coeli

[1] Egerton MSS. 1651, f. i b and N. Lib. 238 i. 12.

2. In quibus luces itidem ut Pyropus
   Nobiles inter radiat lapillos
   Utuc formosus facie inter ardet
                Lucifer astra

3. Jus tibi summum necis atq: vitae
   Tradidit magni moderator orbis
   Tu potes servare probos et idem
                Perdere sontes

4. Tu piorum tutor et advocatus
   Tu Dei in Templo nitidas ad alas
   Visus es dextra tenuisse plenam
                Thuris acerram

5. Inde surgens fumus odore multo
   Ibat ad summi solidum tonantis
   Ac Dei nares liquidi juvabant
                Dona vaporis

6. Tu pias latis animas reponis
   Sedibus olim gelida exciebis
                Funera bustis

7. Quam dedit laetos pia turba plausus
   Cum gravi coelum quateret ruina
   Hostis et serpens veterator acti
                Non sine pugna

8. Illic sublimes subito sub auras
   Emicans septem (stupuere cuncti)
   Ora tollebat colubris tumebant
                Colla trecentis.

9. Flammeis ardens oculis avernum
   Virus efflabat furiale monstrum
   Fulminisq: instar piceos vomebat
                Faucibus ignes

10. Te nihil terret labies minacis
    Beluae sed vi domitam superna
    Cogis absorptam superas ad auras
                  Reddere praedam

11. Quae tuas fulvas fugiat sub alas
    Laeta praesenti sed adhuc periclo
    Palpitans elapsa velut rapaci
                  Ales ab ungui

12. Ergo ne quid jam trepident cadaver
    Triste deturbas, labat, a labantis
    Pondus exhorrens aperit profunda
                  Tartara tellus

13. Non secus quam si Siculo Feloto
    Pendulum in fluctus abeat cacumen
    Territum cedit refluumque late
                  Dissilit aequor

14. Ferreis illic domitus catenis
    Horridum quassat caput ac minatus
    Multo nequicquam furibundus iras
                  Volvit inanes

15. Te manet palma Michael suprema
    Te novi plausus tibi non iniquas
    Impius poenas dabit antichristus
                  Orbe levato

16. Laetus idcirco meritos uterque
    Orbis in hymnos canit altus aether
    Inclyto gaudet duce gaudet aeque
                  Praeside tellus

17. At meri cantus celebrantur isthic
     Hic (uti res sunt variae atque mixtae)
     Reddimus proni quaerulis remixta
                    Carmina votis

18. En vides quantis miseri premamur
     Cladibus (nostro merito fatemur).
     Toto proh caeci terimus nefandis
                    Secula bellis

19. (Si tibi haud frustra data cum nostri est)
     Si tibi per non temere vocablum
     Mutuat belli procul O cruentos
                    Pelle furores

20. Fac tua lenis prece rex olympi
     Vindicum condat miseratus ensem
     Ferias donet referatque fessis
                    Ocia terris

IV

MANUCAPTORS

The Document,[1] of which the following is a faithful transcript is, as stated in its prefatory note, a record of "the amount of all the fines made in the presence of Master Thomas Harryes, King's chaplain, William Hatteclyffe and Roger Holand, the King's Commissioners by divers persons, his subjects, for their contempt against the said King perpetrated, made and committed".

Here for convenience of reference the several items are numbered and indexes are provided at the end both of the

---

[1] The P.R.O. reference is E.101. 516, 27.

manucaptors and of the parishes. The Latin is extended throughout, the only abbreviation being M. for Manucaptore and MM. for Manucaptoribus. Every item presupposes the preposition *de* before it. In the introductory note, the MS of which is torn, the words within the brackets have been supplied from the corresponding Devonshire MS.

(Anno XIIII) Domini nostri Regis
(Henrici ANGLIAE) Septimi

(Comitatus Cornubiae. Onus omnium finium) factorum coram Magistro Thoma Harryes domini Regis capellano, (Willielmo Hatteclyffe) et Rogero Holand ejusdem domini Regis commissionariis per diversos (Suos subditos ibidem) pro contemptu eorum erga dictum Dominum Regem perpetrato, facto et (commisso) prout inferius Patet

Videlicet.

1. De David Moile de Newlyn manucaptore pro
   inhabitantibus parochiae ibidem   £6
2. Domino Thoma Alen vicario de Newlyn   £20
3. Willielmo Trevanion armigero et Thoma
   Hellond de Saint Michaell Careheies MM.
   pro inhabitantibus parochiae ibidem   £10
4. Johanne Goldon de Probus M. pro inhabitantibus parochiae ibidem   £10
5. Johanne Micholl sacrista de Peryn   100s.
6. Petro Harvy ab Trevisek   £3
7. Johanne Wattys et Ede Michell de St Denys
   MM. pro inhabitantibus parochiae ibidem   40s.
8. Johanne Newhale de Bodmin et Richardo
   Wattys de Sancto Laurenc MM. pro inhabitantibus parochiae de Withiell   £4

9. Magistro Willielmo Piers vicario de Brick et
    Johanne Godolphin juniore MM. pro
    inhabitantibus parochiae ibidem cum cap-
    ella de Germowe   4 marks

10. Petro Santaban de Helston et de Monte Mi-
    chaelis M. pro inhabitantibus parochiae de
    Helstonburgh   £4

11. Eodem Petro M. pro inhabitantibus parochiae
    de Sidney   10s.

12. Eodem Petro M. pro inhabitantibus parochiae
    de Crowan   4 marks

13. Thoma Tregos M. pro inhabitantibus paro-
    chiae de Antony   5 marks

¹14. Eodem Thoma M. pro inhabitantibus de
    Sant Ives   10 marks

15. Eodem Thoma M. pro inhabitantibus paro-
    chiae de Managhan   40s.

16. Eodem Thoma M. pro inhabitantibus paro-
    chiae de Constantyn   5 marks

17. Willielmo Trewynnard de St Ergh M. pro
    inhabitantibus parochiae ibidem   40s.

18. Thoma Tregos M. pro inhabitantibus paro-
    chiae de Budok   40s.

19. Domino Willielmo Vicy retore de Landilpa
    M. pro inhabitantibus parochiae ibidem

20. Johanne Bevile de Marques Ewe M. pro in-
    habitantibus villae ibidem et parochiae de
    Sant Hillary   100s.

21. Eodem Johanne M. pro inhabitantibus paro-
    chiae Sancti Pauli   100s.

---

¹ The word Ives is in another's handwriting and should be *Just*.
See No. 28.

22. Johanne Glynne de Bodmyn M. pro inhabi-
    tantibus parochiae et villae ibidem   5 marks
23. Stephano Calmady de Ewny juxta Lanant M.
    pro inhabitantibus parochiae de Ludvan   £4
24. Eodem Stephano M. pro Johanne Tregillowe   5 marks
25. Eodem Stephano M. pro inhabitantibus paro-
    chiae de Uny juxta Lenant et Trewynek   100*s.*
26. Eodem Stephano M. pro inhabitantibus de
    Sant Felix   £4
27. Johanne Tregaso et Johanne Smyth de Lescard
    MM. pro inhabitantibus parochiae et burgi
    de Launceston   £4
[1]28. Johanne Bevile de Marquis Ewe M. pro in-
    habitantibus parochiae de Just in Lenant   4 marks
29. Johanne Cadwodley de Exon M. pro inhabi-
    tantibus parochiae de Sant Kube   4 marks
30. Willielmo Janyn de Mawgan in Pider M. pro
    inhabitantibus parochiae ibidem   106*s.* 8*d.*
31. John Bevile de Lambol M. pro inhabitantibus
    parochiae de Wynvola   40*s.*
32. Johanne Durant de Pensignans M. pro inhabi-
    tantibus parochiae de Gwynnap   £4
33. Eodem Johanne M. pro inhabitantibus de
    Arwothall   26*s.* 8*d.*
34. Eodem Johanne M. pro inhabitantibus paro-
    chiae sive capellae de Stithians   40*s.*
35. Ricardo Code de Morvale M. pro inhabitan-
    tibus parochiae ibidem   100*s.*
36. Ricardo Reynolds de Innoder M. pro inhabi-
    tantibus parochiae ibidem   5 marks

[1] See No. 14.

37. Thoma Basley rectore de Northill M. pro
    inhabitantibus parochiae ibidem   £4

38. Stephano Calmady de Uny Lenant M. pro
    inhabitantibus parochiae de Madron   10 marks

39. Eodem Stephano et Johanne Bevile de Marques
    Ewe MM. pro Mattheo Edmunds 20s.
    Ricardo Petit 100s. et Thoma Nankivell de
    parochia de Madron predicto 40s.   £8

40. Johanne Bevile de Marques Ewe et Thoma
    Tregos de Madron MM. pro Edwardo
    Jamys de eadem   4 marks

41. Johanne Bevile de Marques Ewe et Radulpho
    Milepens de Paullo   4 marks

42. Johanne Bevile de Namboll M. pro inhabitan-
    tibus parochiae de Kenayne   20 marks

43. Willielmo Herrys de Bruerd pro inhabitantibus
    parochiae ibidem   40s.

44. Stephano Calmady de Lenant et Johanne
    Bevile de Marques Ewe MM. pro inhabi-
    tantibus parochiae de Sant Sancrete

45. Willielmo Trewynnard de Trewynnard M.
    pro Domino Thoma Polstrong vicario de
    Ergh   10 marks

46. Stephano Calmady de Lenant et Johanne
    Bevile de Lamboll MM. pro inhabitantibus
    de Boryan   100s.

47. Eisdem Stephano et Johanne MM. pro in-
    habitantibus Capellae de Selleven infra
    parochiam Sancti Boriani   40s.

48. Eisdem Stephano et Johanne MM. pro in-
    habitantibus pertinentibus et incumbentibus
    capellae de Senan   40s.

49. Eisdem Stephano et Johanne MM. pro Ricardo Nicoll Willes de Sellevan   40s.

50. Eisdem Stephano et Johanne pro inhabitantibus parochiae de Sener   40s.

51. Eisdem Stephano et Johanne pro inhabitantibus de Peryn Uthno   40s.

52. Eisdem Stephano et Johanne MM. pro Willielmo Brain (or *Bram*) de Sancrete   40s.

53. Eisdem Stephano et Johanne MM. pro inhabitantibus monlentibus et pertinentibus capellae de Gothian pertinenti parochiae Sant Felicis   26s. 8d.

54. Willielmo Trewynnard de Trewynnard M. pro inhabitantibus parochiae de Gwynnyer   100s.

55. Magistro Alexandro Penhill rectore de Ellogans M. pro inhabitantibus parochiae de Rederhith   £4

56. Eodem Magistro M. pro inhabitantibus parochiae de Sant Logan   5 marks

57. Eodem Magistro Alexandro M. pro inhabitantibus parochiae de Camborne   £4

58. Thoma Penwarne M. pro inhabitantibus parochiae Sant Columb Minore   5 marks

59. Ricardo Conker (or *Couker*) et Johanne de Stoke Climeslond M. pro inhabitantibus parochiae ibidem   100s.

60. Ricardo Code de Morvale M. pro inhabitantibus parochiae de Callant   4 marks

61. Thoma Tregos de Madron M. pro parochia de Mawgan   £4

62. Eodem Thoma M. pro inhabitantibus capellae de Cury annexatae parochiae de Briak   60s.

63. Eodem Thoma M. pro inhabitantibus parochiae de Wyn vola   60s.
64. Thoma Penwarne M. pro inhabitantibus parochiae de Mawnan   40s.
65. Johanne Trevenor de Lamoran M. pro inhabitantibus parochiae ibidem   26s. 8d.
66. Johanne Brandon et Johanne Phillip de Calstok M. pro inhabitantibus parochiae ibidem   10 marks
67. Thoma Harrys et Thoma Pen'ell de Sant Jehon or Jehou M. pro inhabitantibus parochiae ibidem   40s.
68. Frauncisco Jago de Peran in Zabulo M. pro inhabitantibus ibidem   100s.
69. Johanne Trelawny et Johanne Corington MM. pro inhabitantibus de Mynhynnes   10 marks
70. Johanne Bake et Johanne Bedyk de Lanrake MM. pro inhabitantibus parochiae de Lanrake   100s.
71. Ricardo Bonethan et Johanne Jankyn MM. pro inhabitantibus parochiae de Miler   4 marks
72. Thoma Penwarne de Mawnan M. pro inhabitantibus parochiae Ruan Minor   40s.
73. Ricardo Smyth de Sant Jermyns   10 marks
74. Johanne Cosuwarth de Colan M. pro inhabitantibus parochiae ibidem   40s.
75. Thoma Berkeley de Carentok   40s.
76. Johanne Manaton et Nicholas Crabbe de Southill et Kellington   5 marks
77. Willielmo Jeene et Johanne Wolgarne MM. pro inhabitantibus burgi de Launceston   40s.
78. Ricardo Code de Morvale armigero M. pro inhabitantibus parochiae de Keane   40s.

79. Ricardo Comer et Ricardo Stone de Mynvere
    MM. pro inhabitantibus parochiae ibidem 40s.
80. Benedicto Trefrie et Radulpho Ronell de Sant
    Tetha MM. pro inhabitantibus parochiae
    ibidem   40s.
81. Johanne Berkeleyde Mawagan M. pro in-
    habitantibus parochiae ibidem   £4
82. Nicholas Enys de Luxulian M. pro inhabitan-
    tibus parochiae ibidem   40s.
83. Roberto Comer de Dewstowe M. pro inhabi-
    tantibus parochiae ibidem   40s.
84. Willielmo More et Johanne Payne de Altnon
    M. pro inhabitantibus parochiae ibidem   40s.
85. Johanne Hethman de Stoke Clymslond   20s.
86. Johanne Cadley de eadem   40s.
87. Johanne Carew de Maker armigero M. pro
    inhabitantibus parochiae ibidem   4 marks
88. Johanne Carew de Antony M. pro inhabitan-
    tibus parochiae de Rame   40s.
89. Eodem Johanne M. pro inhabitantibus paro-
    chiae de Sant John   26s. 8d.
90. Eodem Johanne M. pro inhabitantibus paro-
    chiae de Antony   5 marks
91. Johanne Bere seniore de Brieke M. pro in-
    habitantibus parochiae ibidem   £4
92. Willielmo Pagett et Willielmo Tregle de
    Eglyshale MM. pro inhabitantibus paro-
    chiae ibidem   4 marks
93. Johanne Lanorwen de Sheviok M. pro inhabi-
    tantibus parochiae ibidem   4 marks
94. Roberto Kellegrew de Sant Ives M. pro in-
    habitantibus parochiae ibidem   100s.

95. Willielmo Trewynnard et Nicholas Enys MM. pro Johanne Tresynny de Penryn burgh   £30

96. Thoma Tregos de Sant Antony et Thoma Budokside de Budok in comitatu Cornubiae armigero MM. pro Domino Nicholao Clyse vicario de Constantyn   10 marks

97. Johanne Nankarowe de Penkevell M. pro inhabitantibus parochiae ibidem   40s.

98. Eodem Johanne M. pro inhabitantibus parochiae de Kenwyn et Merther   40s.

99. Johanne Kyngdon de Quethok M. pro inhabitantibus parochiae ibidem   5 marks

100. Willielmo Trevanion armigero et Thoma Poile de Tregony MM. pro inhabitantibus parochiae ibidem cum capella de Keby eidem annexa   100s.

101. Thoma Mares de Marewike generoso M. pro inhabitantibus parochiae ibidem   5 marks

102. Johanne Corington de Nywton generoso M. pro inhabitantibus parochiae de Melan   40s.

103. Ricardo Code de Morwall M. pro inhabitantibus parochiae de Lansalwys   100s.

104. Ricardo Warde et Willielmo Baldewyn de Pilaton MM. pro inhabitantibus parochiae ibidem   4 marks

105. Nicholao Baudyn de Mabyn M. pro inhabitantibus parochiae ibidem   4 marks

106. Thoma Minster de Norton in parochia de Stoke Clemeslond   26s. 8d.

107. Johanne Worthevale et Johanne Gibbes de Minster MM. pro inhabitantibus parochiae ibidem   4 marks

108. Johanne Genne et Thoma Willes de Kilkington MM. pro inhabitantibus parochiae ibidem — 4 marks

109. Johanne Rowse et Johanne Holman de Warbistowe MM. pro inhabitantibus parochiae ibidem — 40s.

110. Stephano Adam et Johanne Cundy MM. pro inhabitantibus de Sant Genys — 40s.

111. Johanne Corington de Newton M. pro inhabitantibus parochiae de Domynyk — 5 marks

112. Nicholas Enys de Luxulian armigero M. pro Renfrido Enys et Willielmo Penrose — 4 marks

113. Johanne Corington de Newton armigero M. pro inhabitantibus parochiae de Lankynhorne — 40s.

114. Thoma Lescawyn et Waltero Downynd de Lewannak MM. pro inhabitantibus parochiae ibidem — 5 marks

115. Thoma Smyth et Johanne Merefeld de Launstonland MM. pro inhabitantibus parochiae ibidem — 40s.

116. Ricardo Denys et Johanne Duxton de Boyton MM. pro inhabitantibus parochiae ibidem — 40s.

117. Johanne Cundy et Waltero Cokke de Julet MM. pro inhabitantibus parochiae ibidem — 40s.

118. Johanne Langdon de Kev'ell et Johanne Calf de Loghe MM. pro inhabitantibus parochiae de Martyn de Loghe — 5 marks

119. Johanne Tresynny de Penryn burgh M. pro inhabitantibus parochiae de Petrok parva, — 26s. 8d.

120. Johanne Whiete et Johanne Yoge de Dulo MM. pro inhabitantibus parochiae ibidem — 40s.

121. Thoma Trewynnek et Johanne Paulle de
     South Pederwyn MM. pro inhabitantibus
     parochiae ibidem   40s.
122. Magistro Alexandro Penhill et Thoma Tre-
     wynnek MM. pro inhabitantibus paro-
     chiae de Lawhitton   4 marks
123. Willielmo Kelly de Ponstoke M. pro inhabi-
     tantibus parochiae ibidem   40s.
124. Johanne Skeye et Thoma Jule de Cleder
     MM. pro inhabitantibus parochiae ibidem 40s.
125. Thoma Penwarne de Mawnan M. pro in-
     habitantibus parochiae de Melian   5 marks
126. Johanne Hiden de Jacobstow et Sacho
     Warde MM. pro inhabitantibus ibidem   40s.
127. Johanne Behethelyn de Penrynburgh et
     Gluvias M. pro inhabitantibus parochiae
     ibidem   10 marks
128. Radulpho Tresaluest de Sant Wenn M. pro
     inhabitantibus parochiae ibidem   26s. 8d.
129. Nicholas Rowe et Johanne Trewassa de
     Treneglos MM. pro inhabitantibus paro-
     chiae ibidem   40s.
130. Roberto Herby de Erbyn M. pro inhabitanti-
     bus parochiae ibidem   40s.
131. Johanne Trevathan de Erme M. pro inhabi-
     tantibus parochiae ibidem   40s.
132. Willielmo Rawlyn et Radulpho Stephen de
     Elerky sive Seberrian MM. pro inhabi-
     tantibus parochiae ibidem   40s.
133. Johanne Trewortha et Johanne Trecreke de
     Ruan MM. pro inhabitantibus paro-
     chiae ibidem   40s.

134. Johanne Pelyne et Johanne Medros de
Geryns MM. pro inhabitantibus paro-
chiae ibidem   40s.

135. Alexandro Laurence et Georgio Toine de
Egloskerise (Eglosrose) alias File M. pro
inhabitantibus parochiae ibidem   4 marks

136. Johanne Coriton de Pynnok M. pro inhabitantibus parochiae ibidem   40s.

137. Henrico Berwike et Thoma Treoarn de
Trevelga MM. pro inhabitantibus parochiae ibidem   40s.

138. Willielmo Dier et Johanne Landton de Marhamchurch MM. pro inhabitantibus parochiae ibidem   40s.

139. Stephano Dogowe et Reginaldo Laurence de
Roche MM. pro inhabitantibus parochiae
ibidem   40s.

140. Johanne Croseman de Bowfleming M. pro
inhabitantibus parochiae ibidem   40s.

141. Johanne Wolgarne de Launceston M. pro
inhabitantibus parochiae de Egloskery   40s.

142. Johanne Cragowe de Sant Pynnok et Johanne Wolgarne de Launceston MM.
pro inhabitantibus parochiae de Boconok   40s

143. Hugone Trethirf de Ladoc M. pro inhabitantibus parochiae ibidem   40s.

144. Francisco Parker et Willielmo Launce de
Clements MM. pro inhabitantibus parochiae ibidem   40s.

145. Johanne Browncose et Michaele Marrok de
Kee MM. pro inhabitantibus parochiae
ibidem   40s.

146. David Tailor et Thoma Harrys de Lostu-
     thiel MM. pro inhabitantibus parochiae
     ibidem   £4
147. Hugone Tretherf de Ladoc M. pro Ricardo
     Alyn de eadem capellano   40s.
148. Roberto Myngose et Johanne Huchen de
     Blasy MM. pro inhabitantibus parochiae
     ibidem   4 marks
149. Thoma Bevile de Trurue M. pro inhabitan-
     tibus parochiae de Alyn   4 marks
150. Eodem Thoma M. pro inhabitantibus paro-
     chiae de Feoke   40s.
151. Thoma Mille et Thoma Honning de White-
     stan MM. pro inhabitantibus parochiae
     ibidem   40s.
152. Willielmo Symonds et Johanne Hendre MM.
     pro inhabitantibus parochiae de Tyndagell 40s.
153. Thoma Talcarne et Waltero Cranberry MM.
     pro inhabitantibus parochiae de Poghill   40s.
154. Johanne Colles de North Tanton M. pro
     inhabitantibus parochiae de Stratton   40s.
155. Willielmo Trevanyon armigero et Johanne
     Wolgarne MM. pro inhabitantibus paro-
     chiae de Lanrethewy   4 marks
156. Ricardo Davy et Stephano Andriwe de Bro-
     thok MM. pro inhabitantibus parochiae
     ibidem   40s.
157. Roberto Batyn de Sant Genys M. pro in-
     habitantibus parochiae de Ottram   20s.
158. Johanne David de Grauntpound et Johanne
     Canarder de Trevelas pro inhabitantibus
     parochiae de Creda   4 marks

159. Petro Noell et Johanne Godak de Antony
MM. pro inhabitantibus parochiae ibi-
dem   20s.

160. Johanne William et Johanne Bossethowe de
Mewan MM. pro inhabitantibus paro-
chiae ibidem   40s.

161. Jankyn Borsaberdewe de Ewny Lenant   5 marks

162. Viviano Penwarne et Pascasio Nansak de
Just in Rousseland MM. pro inhabitanti-
bus parochiae ibidem   4 marks

163. Pascasio Nansak predicto   10 marks

164. Willielmo Lowre de Sant Wennowe M. pro
inhabitantibus parochiae ibidem   £10

165. Johanne Hawes et Johanne Treyer de Ewa
MM. pro inhabitantibus parochiae ibidem 40s.

166. Eisdem Johanne et Johanne MM. pro inhabitantibus parochiae de Mebagisy   40s.

167. Willielmo Lowre de Wennowe M. pro inhabitantibus de Sant Vape   £4

168. Eodem Willielmo M. pro inhabitantibus
parochiae sive villae de Tywordrath cum
Sant Sampson   £6

169. Alexandro Arundell de Morstow M. pro inhabitantibus parochiae ibidem   £4

170. Magistro Alexandro Penhill rectore de Illogan M. pro inhabitantibus parochiae de
Grade   40s.

171. Eodem Magistro Alexandro M. pro inhabitantibus parochiae Sancti Stephani de
Branell   4 marks

172. Ricardo Code et Johanne Trewynnard MM.
pro inhabitantibus de Warlegon   4 marks

173. Eisdem Ricardo et Johanne MM. pro in-
     habitantibus parochiae de Nyot   4 marks
174. Eisdem Ricardo et Johanne MM. pro in-
     habitantibus parochiae de Lanteglos   4 marks
175. Eisdem Ricardo et Johanne MM. pro inha-
     bitantibus parochiae de Fowey   4 marks
176. Eisdem Ricardo et Johanne MM. pro in-
     habitantibus parochiae de Goran   4 marks
177. Magistro Alexandro Penhill rectore de Lo-
     gan M. pro inhabitantibus parochiae de
     Gwendron   40s.
178. Eodem Magistro Alexandro et Ricardo
     David de Sant Agnes MM. pro inhabitan-
     tibus parochiae ibidem   5 marks
· 179. Johanne Sampson et Thoma Lamolkyn de
     Evalle MM. pro inhabitantibus parochiae
     ibidem   26s. 8d.
180. Eisdem Johanne et Thoma pro inhabitanti-
     bus parochiae de Sant Isye   26s. 8d.
181. Thoma Porkgwinne de Tam'ton M. pro in-
     habitantibus parochiae ibidem   26s. 8d.
182. Johanne Calebodlegh de Exon M. pro in-
     habitantibus parochiarum de Helland et
     Lesnoweth   40s.
183. Johanne Jak Andriwe de Just in Rousland £4
184. Clemente Alyn de eadem   £4

        Summa totalis hujus oneris DCXXIII lib

                Thomas Harryes
                Willms Hatteclyff
                Rogr Holand

Indexes of the Document of 1499

NAMES OF PERSONS

Adam, Stephen, 110
Alen, Thomas, 2
Alyn, Clement, 184
Andriwe, John Jack, 183
Andriwe, Stephen, 156
Arundell, Alexander, 169

Bake, John, 70
Baldewyn, William, 104
Basley, Thomas, 37
Batyn, Robert, 157
Baudyn, Nicholas, 105
Bedyk, John, 70
Behethelyn, John, 127
Bere, John, 91
Berkeley, John, 81
Berkeley, Thomas, 75
Berwike, Henry, 137
Bevile, John (of Lambol), 31, 42
Bevile, John (of Marazion), 20, 21,
    28, 39, 40, 41, 44, 46, 47, 48, 49,
    50, 51, 52, 53
Bevile, Thomas, 149, 150
Bonethon, Richard, 71
Borsaberdewe, Jankyn, 161
Bossethowe, John, 160
Brain (or Bram), William, 52
Brandon, John, 66
Brownecose, John, 145
Budokside, Thomas, 96

Cadley, John, 86
Cadwodley, John, 29
Calebodlegh, John, 182
Calf, John, 118
Calmady, Stephen, 23, 24, 25, 26,
    38, 39, 44, 46, 47, 48, 49, 50, 51,
    52, 53

Canarder, John, 158
Carew (of Antony), John, 88, 89,
    90
Carew (of Maker), John, 87
Cock, Walter, 117
Code, Richard, 35, 60, 78, 103,
    172, 173, 174, 175, 176
Colles, John, 154
Comer, Richard, 79
Comer, Robert, 83
Conker (or Couker), Richard, 59
Corington (Coriton), John, 69,
    102, 111, 113, 136
Cosuwarth, John, 74
Crabbe Nicholas, 76
Cragowe, John, 142
Cranberry, Walter, 153
Croseman, John, 140
Cundy, John, 110, 117

David, John, 158
David, Richard, 178
Davy, Richard, 156
Denys, Richard, 116
Dier, William, 138
Dogowe, Stephen, 139
Downynd, Walter, 114
Durant, John, 32, 33, 34
Duxton, John, 116

Edmunds, Matthew, 39
Enys, Nicholas, 82, 95, 112
Enys, Remfry, 112

Genne, John, 108
Gibbes, John, 107
Glynne, John, 22
Godak, John, 159

Godolphin, John, 9
Goldon, John, 4

Harris, Thomas, 67, 146
Harvy, Peter, 6
Hawes, John, 165, 166
Hellond, Thomas, 3
Hendre, John, 152
Herby, Robert, 130
Herrys, Thomas, 67
Herrys, William, 43
Hethman, John, 85
Hiden, John, 126
Holman, John, 109
Honnyng, Thomas, 151
Huchen, John, 148

Jago, Francis, 68
Jamys, Edward, 40
Jankyn, John, 71
Janyn, William, 30
Jeene, William, 77
Jule, Thomas, 124

Kellegrewe, Robert, 94
Kelly, William, 123
Kyngdon, John, 99

Lamolkyn, Thomas, 179, 180
Landton, John, 138
Langdon, John, 118
Lanorwen, John, 93
Launce, William, 144
Laurence, Alexander, 135
Lawrence, Reginald, 139
Lescawyn, Thomas, 114
Lower, William, 164, 167, 168

Manaton, John, 76
Mares, Thomas, 101
Marrok, Michael, 145
Medro, John, 134
Merefeld, John, 115
Micholl, John, 5
Milepens, Ralph, 41

Mille, Thomas, 151
Minster, Thomas, 106
Moile, David, 1
More, William, 84
Myngose, Robert, 148

Nankarowe, John, 97, 98
Nankevill, Thomas, 39
Nansok, Pascoe, 162, 163
Newhale, John, 8
Noell, Peter, 159

Pagett, William, 92
Parker, Francis, 144
Paulle, John, 121
Payne, John, 84
Pelyne, John, 134
Pen'ell, Thomas, 67
Penhill, Alexander, 55, 56, 57, 122,
    170, 171, 177, 178
Penrose, William, 112
Penwarne, Thomas, 58, 64, 72,
    125
Penwarne, Vivian, 162
Petit, Richard, 39
Phillip, John, 66
Piers, William, 9
Poile, Thomas, 100
Polstrong, Thomas, 45
Porkgwynne, Thomas, 181

Rawlyn, William, 132
Reynolds, Richard, 36
Ronell, Ralph, 80
Rowe, Nicholas, 129
Rowse, John, 109

St Aubyn (Santaban), Peter, 10,
    11, 12
Sampson, John, 179, 180
Skeye, John, 124
Smyth, John, 27
Smyth, Richard, 73
Smyth, Thomas, 115
Stephen, Ralph, 132

Stone, Richard, 79
Symonds, William, 152

Tailor, David, 146
Talcarne, Thomas, 153
Toine, George, 135
Trecreke, John, 133
Trefrie, Benedict, 80
Tregaso, John, 27
Tregillowe, John, 24
Tregle, William, 92
Tregos, Thomas, 13, 14, 15, 16, 18, 40, 61, 62, 63, 96
Trelawny, John, 69
Treoarn, Thomas, 137
Tresalvestor, Ralph, 128
Tresynny, John, 119
Trethirf, Hugh, 143, 147
Trevanion, William, 3, 100, 155
Trevathan, John, 131
Trevenor, John, 65
Trewassa, John, 129

Trewortha, John, 133
Trewynnard, John, 172, 173, 174, 175, 176
Trewynnard, William, 17, 45, 54, 95
Trewynnek, Thomas, 121, 122
Treyer, John, 165, 166

Vicy, William, 19

Ward, Richard, 104
Ward, Sacho, 126
Wattys, John, 7
Wattys, Richard, 8
Whiete, John, 120
Willes, Richard Nicoll, 49
Willes, Thomas, 108
William, John, 160
Wolgarne, John, 77, 141, 142, 155
Worthevale, John, 107

Yoge, John, 120

PARISHES

Advent
St Agnes, 178
St Allen, 149
Altarnun, 84
St Anthony in Meneage, 13
St Anthony in Roseland, 159
Antony, 90
St Austell

St Blazey, 148
Blisland
Boconnoc, 142
Bodmin, 8, 22
Botus Fleming, 140
Boyton, 116
Bradoc, 156

Breage, 9, 62
St Breock, 91
St Breward, 43
Bridgerule
Budock, 18, 96
St Buryan, 46

Caerhayes, 3
Callington, 76
Calstock, 66
Camborne, 57
Cardynham
St Cleer
St Clement, 144
St Clether, 124
Colan, 74

St Columb Major
St Columb Minor, 58
Constantine, 16, 96
Cornelly
Crantock, 75
Creed, 158
Crowan, 12
Cubert, 29. See 100
Cuby, 100
Cury, 62

Davidstow, 83
St Denys, 7
St Dominic, 111
Duloe, 120

Egloshayle, 92
Egloskerry, 141
Endellion
St Enoder, 36
St Erme, 131
St Erth, 17, 45
St Ervan, 130
St Eval, 179
St Ewe, 165

St Feock, 150
Forrabury
Fowey, 175

St Gennys, 110, 157
St Germans, 73
St Germoe, 9
St Gerrans, 134
St Gluvias, 127
St Gluvias, Penryn, 95, 119
St Goran, 176
St Grade, 170
Gulval
Gunwallow, 63
Gwennap, 32
Gwinear, 54
Gwithian, 53

Helland, 182

Helston, 10
St Hilary, 20

Illogan, 56
St Isseu, 180
St Ives, 14, 94. See 28

Jacobstow, 126
St John, 67 (?), 89
St Juliot, 117
St Just in Penwith, 14
St Just in Roseland, 162, 163, 183,
    184

Kea, 145
Kenwyn, 42 (?), 98
St Keverne, 42
St Keverne, Namboli, 31
St Kew
St Keyne, 78
Kilkhampton, 108

Ladock, 143, 147
Lamorran, 65
Landewednack, 31
Landrake, 70
Landulph, 19
Laneast
Lanhydrock
Lanivet
Lanlivery
Lanreath, 155
Lansallos, 103
Lanteglos by Camelford.   See
    174
Lanteglos by Fowey, 174
Launcells
Launceston, 27, 77. See 27, 115
St Laurence, 8
Lawhitton, 122
Lelant, 25, 161
Lesnewth, 182
St Levan, 47, 49
Lewannick, 114
Lezant

Linkinhorne, 113
Liskeard, 27
Little Petherick, 119
Lostwithiel, 146
Ludgvan, 23
Luxulyan, 82, 112

Mabe
St Mabyn, 105
Madron, 38, 39, 40
Maker, 87
Manacean, 15
Marhamchurch, 138
St Martin by Looe, 118
St Martin in Meneage
St Mawgan in Meneage, 61
St Mawgan in Pydar, 30, (81?)
Mawnan, 64, 125
St Mellion, 102. See 125
Menheniot, 69
St Merryn
Merther, 98
Mevagissey, 166
St Mewan, 160
St Michael Caerhayes, 3
St Michael Penkivel, 97
St Michael's Mount, 10
Michaelstow
Minster, 107
St Minver, 79
Morvah
Morval, 35, 78
Morwenstow, 169
Mullyan, 125
Mylor, 71

St Neot, 173
Newlyn, 1, 2
North Hill, 37
North Petherwyn

Otterham, 157

Padstow
Paul, 21, 41

Pelynt
Penryn, 95
Perran an Worthal, 33
Perran Uthnoe, 51
Perran Zabuloe, 68
Phillack, 26
Philleigh, 135
Pillaton, 104
St Pinnock, 136
Poughill, 153
Poundstock, 123
Probus, 4

Quethiock, 99

Rame, 88
Redruth, 55
Roche, 139
Ruan Lanihorne, 133
Ruan Major, 133
Ruan Minor, 72

St Sampson, 168
Sancreed, 44, 52 (?)
Sennen, 48
Sheviocke, 93
Sithney, 11
South Hill with Callington, 76
South Petherwyn, 121
St Stephens in Brannel, 171
St Stephens by Launceston, 67
    (?)
St Stephens, Saltash, 67 (?)
Stoke Climsland, 59, 85, 106
Stratton, 154
Stythians, 34

Talland, 60
Tamerton, 181
St Teath, 80
Temple
St Thomas
Tintagel, 152
Towednack, 25
Tregony, 100

Treneglos, 129
Tresmere
Trevalga, 137
Truro, 149
St Tudy
Tywardreath, 168

St Veep, 167
Veryan, 132

Warbstow, 109
Warleggan, 172
Week St Mary, 101
Wendron, 177
St Wenn, 128
Whitstone, 151
St Winnow, 164, 167
Withiel, 8

Zennor, 50

Note—In this index it has been thought good to include all the parishes in Cornwall although some of them are not directly referred to in the assessment. The reasons for their omission are not evident, but in some cases it is possible to suggest an explanation, e.g. Advent, Cornelly and Mabe were chapelries and included in their mother parishes; Egloshayle, Gulval, St Kew and Lezant belonged to the Bishop; St Austell and Padstow were monastic lands and St Endellion collegiate; Blislaud was in the King's hands and Cardynham had been given by him to the Lord Treasurer.

GENERAL INDEX

Arscott, John, archpriest, 78
Arundell, Humphry, 91–100
Arundell, Sir John, 3, 4, 130

Basset, Arthur, 167
Basset, Sir Francis, 90, 162–167
Basset, *Letters*, 165, 166
Bells, 7–9
Benedictines, 36, 37
Bevill, John, 149
Bevill, Peter, 4, 148
Birinus, archbishop, 75
Blake, Mr W. J., ix
Bloyou, Ralph, 46, 117, 145
Bodmin, mayor and miller of, 99
Bodrugan, Henry, 129, 133, 134
Borlase, Dr William, 3, 4
Botreaux (de Boterels), Reginald, 116
Breakwater, 72
Brismar the Priest, 25
Brittany, Alan, count of, 40
Bronze Age, 21
Brychan, 74
Buckland, Mr C. B., xi

Cadoc, Saint, 22
Carew, Richard, x, 97–99
Carnepyssack's rebellion, 91–92
Cassiterides, 14
Chevy Chase room, frieze of, 9
Clyst Heath, 95
Cornwall, Reginald, earl of, 112
Cornwall, Rohesia, the earl's sister, 113

Delehaye, Father, S.J., ix, 18
Dinsol, 22
Diodorus Siculus, 13

Duchess of Cornwall's Progress, 141
Dunstanville, Alan de, 115

Earthquake, 3
Edgcombe, Sir Peter, 138
Edgcombe, Sir Richard, 133
Edward the Confessor, 23, 24, 31
Erasmus, 27
  his epigram, App. II
Étaples, Treaty of, 135
Exeter, Assault of, 138

Fencibles, 160
Flamank, Thomas, 136
Fortescue, Sir John, 128

Glastonbury, 25
Gordon, Lady Catherine, 135, 139, 140
Great Rebellion, 164–168
Gregory, Pope, 102, 103, App. I

Harris family, 153–158
  pedigree, 154
Henry VI, miracles, 88
  spurs and sword, 87
Herepath (Harepath), Richard, 61
Hermits, 23
Herodotus, 12
Hilda, abbess, 76

Ictis, 11–20
Inventories, 54, 66, 80–86

Knights Hospitallers, 5, 115

Lambessow, 39
Legenda Aurea, ix, 18, 19
Leland, John, 2

Leofric, Bishop, his charters, 102, 103, App. I
Lisle, Honor, viscountess, 151
Loth, Professor J., 43

Madron, 6
Manucaptors, 142, App. III
Marazion, 46, 47
Meneage, 30
Milleton (Melyton), John, 152
Milleton (Melyton), William, 89, 152
Mont St Michel, 31, 38, 63, 119
Mortain, count of, 31–34
Morton, William, 65, 69–74, 147

Nonnita, Saint, 75
Norden, John, 4

Oliver, Dr George, 34
Oxford, John, earl of, 103

Paul, Rev. F. W., xi
Phoenicians, 14, 16, 17
Pliny (the elder), 15
Pomeray (de la Pomerai) arms, 114
Pomeray, Henry, 112, 114, 115
Pomeray, Jollan, 113
Posidonius, 13
Pytheas the Navigator, 17

Read, Mr Clement, ix, 11
Reredos of alabaster, 5
Rickard, Mr T. A., ix, 11, 15
Roger, abbot, 84
Roses, Wars of the, 122
Roseworthy, 112, 115

St Aubyn, arms, 171
St Aubyn, Colonel John, 9, 90, 162–170

St Aubyn, Peter, 148, 150
St Aubyn, Thomas, 148, 151
St Hilary, 8, 9
St Levan, Lord, xi, 170
St Michael, Apparitions of, 26, 27, 29
St Michael, Chair of, 4, 105, 106
St Michael, Light of, 4
St Michael's Mount, 1–10
    Appropriation to Syon, 65
    Fairs of, 40, 41
    Lease of, 151
    Markets of, 45
    Notification, 35
    Purchase of, 162
    Siege of, 127
    Tithe of fish, 49–51
    Tithe of land, 47, 48
Salisbury, Robert, earl of, 88, 90, 160, 163
Salisbury, William, earl of, 162
Simnel, Lambert, 134
Smith, Mr Reginald, 11
Strabo, 14

Traboe, 33, 89
Treiwel (Truthwall), 32
Trevarthian corody, 110
Trewinnard, Deiphobus, 60 *n.*
Trewinnard, Roger, 59
Tristan and Iseult, 42, 43, 97

Virgil, Polydore, x

Wake, Miss Joan, xi
Warkworth, John, x
Warwick, Edward, earl of, 133
Whitsand Bay, 137
Wilfrid, Bishop, 76
Wolsey, Cardinal, 79
Worcester, William of, ix, 18, 27, 74

For EU product safety concerns, contact us at Calle de José Abascal, 56–1°,
28003 Madrid, Spain or eugpsr@cambridge.org.

www.ingramcontent.com/pod-product-compliance
Ingram Content Group UK Ltd.
Pitfield, Milton Keynes, MK11 3LW, UK
UKHW040615240426
470322UK00010B/140